Secrets of RVing on Social Security

Secrets of RVing on Social Security

Jerry Minchey

www.LifeRV.com

Minchey, Jerry. Secrets of RVing on Social Security
How to Enjoy the Motorhome and RV Lifestyle While Living on Your Social Security Income
/ Jerry Minchey

ISBN 978-0-9844968-6-0

1. Recreational vehicle living.

Published by Stony River Media
Knoxville, Tennessee
StonyRiverMedia.com

I am indebted to Patricia Benton, Marilyn Minchey, and Brent Minchey without whose editing, proofing, and formatting this book would not exist.

Contents

Introduction

"If you are lucky enough to find a way of life you love, you have to find the courage to live it."

~ John Irving

Have you ever been driving down the road and met a motorhome and thought, Wouldn't it be nice to just get into one of those RVs, leave all of the yard work or condo-commotion behind, and travel, and live carefree?

Yea, that would be nice if you could afford it, you might be thinking, but that lifestyle is for rich people.

The truth is that motorhome and RV retirement living is one of the most enjoyable and least expensive way to retire, and most people can afford it—even if their only income is their Social Security check.

The purpose of this book is to give you the information to prove to you that this statement is true, and then to show you how you can make it happen.

You can spend a lot of money living the RV lifestyle, but you don't have to. In this book, I'm going to give you the numbers and show you that you can do it all just on your Social Security income. This will include campground fees, gas, and all of your living expenses.

With $1,000 a month income, you can make it happen. Many people spend less than that.

In this book I'll also talk about what's called "boondocking" (which means you are camping for free) and "workamping™" (which is a way to do some volunteer work and get free camping, and sometimes a salary in addition to free camping).

Most RVers do these things part of the time and some do them all of the time. This book covers all of this and more and gives you the inside information RVers are using to live the fun, adventurous, and carefree lifestyle called full-time RVing.

RV life can be expensive if you travel every day, eat out all of the time, and do all of the tourist things. To keep your costs down, you have to remember that you're not on a permanent vacation; this is the way you live.

By the way, the terms "RV" and "motorhome" are used interchangeably by most people. I will generally use the term RV throughout this book to describe both the towable and the drivable types of RV. Sometimes I will use the term motorhome just for variation.

Another term to be aware of is the word, "toad." While boaters call the little boat that they tie behind their big boat a dinghy, RVers call the car they tow behind their motorhome a toad. After all, it is the car that's being "towed."

The appeal and dream of hitting the road has not changed much since the first RVs were introduced back about 1910. Freedom, adventure, fun, and relaxing are words RV owners frequently use to describe why they enjoy the RV lifestyle.

RVing is a low-stress, simplified way of life

Did you ever see an RV parked in front of a psychiatrist's office?

To me, living full time in an RV is a way to live a low-stress, simplified life that has an extra benefit of being very inexpensive. I also find that being part of a community of people who want to do things and go places keeps me feeling young, and it keeps me active.

When you ask people what they would like to do when they retire, many of them say that they want to travel. But conventional travel consisting of airplanes, hotels, motels, car rentals, restaurants, etc., can quickly deplete a nest egg. And on top of that, it's tiring and stressful.

Compare that to the simplified, low-cost, and relaxing lifestyle of living full time in an RV, and sleeping in your own bed, while you travel. If this intrigues you, keep reading.

Is the RV lifestyle the right choice for you?

First of all, living full time in an RV is not necessarily better or worse than how you're living now, it's just different. It's different in a fun, exciting, and adventuresome way. It's a lifestyle many people love, but it's not for everyone.

Many people, as they approach retirement, look forward to traveling, having freedom, enjoying adventure, and being around other people who are doing interesting things. In other words, they don't want a boring life. They want to experience something exciting and different.

And, of course, they want to do all of this well within their budget. That's one of the biggest advantages of living full time in an RV. The RV lifestyle really is one of the least expensive ways to live.

I'm sure you have a lot of questions, and there are many things you want to know about the cost and what's involved in this lifestyle. A lot of this book is about retiring on a much lower budget than most people think about when they think about living full time in an RV.

I will mainly be talking about used RVs in the $5,000 to $25,000 range. I know that's a wide range and, yes, you can find nice RVs in the $5,000 range. Regardless of what you can afford, I highly recommend that you don't buy a new RV as your first RV. I will go into the reasons why later in the book.

Living full time in an RV may be ideal for you and it may not. Making your decision on whether you want to live full time in an RV (and which type of RV) gets easier the more information you have access to. Consider your decision making process and your RV selection process as an adventure, and enjoy the journey.

While living full time in an RV, I have experienced much more excitement and adventure than I ever imagined when I set out on this lifestyle. To me the freedom and flexibility are the best parts. On top of that, as I've said, it's very relaxing, low-stress, and inexpensive.

I also love being around the like-minded and interesting people I meet. I have more friends now than I ever had in my previous lifestyle. I find that I have a lot in common with my new friends. The things I had in common with my previous friends were that we worked together or lived near each other or attended the same church, but not so much because we had any or many common interests. I still stay in touch with many of my former friends, and maybe even more so than before—just not face to face.

A lot of people live their lives hating their jobs, but they go on meeting their obligations and conforming to what society expects from them. What they long for is a life of adventure and travel. In other words, what they really want is freedom.

Now that you're retired (or about to retire), it's a good time to stop and think about how you want to live the next phase of your life. You have the opportunity to live a life of adventure and travel—even if you're living only on your Social Security income. This book will show you how.

Some people make things happen, some people watch things happen, and some people wonder what happened. I think you'll find that the people you meet in campgrounds are the ones who make things happen. After all, if they had not made decisions and made things happen, they wouldn't be in a campground living the RV lifestyle. Continue reading and let me show you how you can be one of them.

Note: Each chapter in this book more or less stands on its own, so you don't have to read them in order. You can skip around and read the chapters you find most interesting first and then come back and read the other chapters later.

I do recommend that you check out the videos and links in each chapter, either as you read through the chapter or by stopping at the end of each chapter to go back and check out the links at that point. You will need to visit the links to get the full understanding and benefit of the content in the chapter in most cases.

Chapter 1

Find out How Much Your Social Security Will Be

"I'm going to retire and live off my savings. What I'll do the next day, I have no idea."

~ Author Unknown

Nothing could be more boring than talking about Social Security rules and numbers, so feel free to skip this chapter for now and maybe come back and read it later.

This is particularly true if you're already drawing your Social Security and already know how much you're receiving each month.

If you're impatient and just want a ballpark number, here it is. As of January 2016 the government reports that **the average person receiving a Social Security check gets $1,341 a month**. You may receive more than this or less.

(That makes sense. That's why it's called an average.) If you want to know exactly how much you will be receiving, keep reading.

If you're not drawing your Social Security yet and want to know more about how much you will be drawing when you start receiving your benefits, I'll try to make this as short and painless as possible.

The first step in finding out if you can comfortably live the RV lifestyle on your Social Security income is to find out how much income you will have to work with.

Of course, if you're already drawing your Social Security payments, you already know how much you're receiving each month, but if you haven't started drawing your payments yet, let me show you how to quickly and easily find out how much you will be drawing.

Then you will know how much you have to work with and we can work and plan from there.

Do you qualify to draw Social Security?

The first thing to do is to make sure you qualify to receive Social Security benefits based on your own work. This is one of the few straight forward answers in the Social Security rule book. To receive Social Security benefits, you must have worked for at least 40 quarters during your lifetime (and earned $1,220 or more in each quarter—indexed to today's numbers). By the way, if you worked for 10 years straight, that would be 40 quarters.

The 40 quarters do not have to be consecutive. These 40 quarters have to be where Social Security Payroll taxes (also known as FICA) were deducted. Of course, you also have to be at least 62 years old before you can start receiving your benefits.

To find out exactly how much your Social Security benefits will be, you can either go to your local Social Security office (plan on being there for an hour or two) or you can go to the government website at http://www.ssa.gov/myaccount and go through the steps of setting up your account. This will only take a few minutes.

You may get slightly different numbers by using the online tool vs. going to the Social Security office in person, but the numbers should be pretty close.

Both of these options will take some time and you may not want to stop and do either one of them right this minute, so let's go on with some general information.

After you've worked enough to qualify for Social Security benefits, your spouse (and/or ex-spouse) may be able to receive Social Security benefits, too, based on your work record. (When they receive benefits, it will not change how much you receive in any way).

There's another side to this. You may be able to receive payments based on the work record of your spouse or ex-spouse.

How is your Social Security payment determined?

When you visit your local Social Security office they will tell you (or when you use the website referred to above, it will calculate) the monthly payment amount for you, but here, in a nutshell, is how the amount is determined:

They take the payroll and self-employment income you earned each year you worked (up to what is called the "tax max," which was $118,500 in 2015, but of course, was a lot less in previous years).

They take the amount you made (and paid Social Security on) each year and then they index each year to account for inflation. For example, if you made $25,000 in 1980, they would multiply that by 3.5 and count it as $87,500 in today's dollars. Then they take the 35 years with the highest indexed earnings and average these and then divide this number by 12 to determine your Average Indexed Monthly Earnings, or AIME.

The government loves to use acronyms. The next two acronyms we'll talk about are PIA and FRA. PIA stands for your Primary Insurance Amount. That's the amount you would be eligible to receive when you reach Full Retirement Age, or FRA as they call it. Below are the numbers showing what Social Security calls your FRA or, in other words, the age when you can start drawing your full retirement amount.

When can you start drawing your Social Security?

You can start collecting at age 62, but at what age can you start drawing your full benefit?

If you were born between 1943 and 1954, your Full Retirement Age is 66. If you were born in 1955 or later, see the information below:

1955 – 66 and 2 months

1957 – 66 and 4 months

1958 – 66 and 6 months

1958 – 66 and 8 months

1959 – 66 and 10 months ✓

1960 and later – 67

You don't have to wait until you reach your full retirement age to start drawing Social Security benefits. You can start at age 62, but you won't receive as much each month as you would if you waited until you reached your full retirement age.

Something to consider: The amount you will receive each month will continue to go up until you reach age 70. After that it doesn't go up any more, so by all means, apply and start receiving your payments no later than when you turn 70.

Here's one other point: In an effort to encourage you to continue working and paying into Social Security, your earnings are not indexed after age 60. What this means is that the money you make after age 60 will be worth more in calculating your Social Security payments.

One final thing to consider is that the longer you can put off drawing your Social Security, the more you will receive in your lifetime assuming you live to the average age.

You might say, "All of that's interesting, but I want to take what I can get now and hit the road. That's why I'm reading this book."

If you're drawing Social Security and still working, your Social Security benefits may be reduced—depending on how much you're making. There are two trigger points to be aware of. If your full retirement age (FRA) is 66 and you are between 62 and 66 and earn more than $15,720 (this is for 2015), your Social Security payment will be reduced by $1 for every $2 you make over the $15,720 amount. Note that investment income and your pension income don't count. It's only your earned income amount that you have to worry about.

During the year you turn 66, your benefits would be reduced by $1 for every $3 you earn over $41,880 (for 2015) and only the months before you turned 66 would be counted. This sounds complicated, but, basically, it means you get to earn more without losing benefits during the year you turn 66.

After you reach your full retirement age (66 plus a few months in most cases), there is no penalty for earning money. You can make as much as you want to and still draw your full Social Security payments.

Do you have to pay income taxes on your Social Security?

I'm not an accountant and the following information is only my understanding of the tax laws. You may owe federal tax on half of your Social Security benefits if your income is $25,000 to $34,000 ($32,000 to $44,000 for joint filers). If you make more than these amounts, you may owe income taxes on up to 85% of your benefits. These are general guidelines. Be sure to follow the instructions on your tax forms or the advice of your tax professional.

A strategy to have your cake and eat it, too

As I said, I'm not an accountant, so get help and advice from a professional to help you implement this strategy, but here's the way I understand how you can combine two features of the Social Security law to maximize what you get:

1. If you delay drawing your Social Security until you reach age 70, your benefits will be 76% higher than if you started drawing at age 62.

2. You can receive benefits based on the work record of your spouse.

Given these two facts, consider this approach: If you and your spouse are about the same age and had about the same income, when you both turned 62, you could each start drawing benefits based on the other person's earnings record.

By doing this and not drawing based on your own earnings, your benefits would continue to increase so that when you do start drawing based on your own earnings at either your full retirement age or at age 70, you would receive a much larger monthly payment.

In the meantime you would each be receiving a reduced monthly benefit by drawing an income based on the earnings of the other spouse. All of the money you receive while you wait to draw the maximum benefits from your own retirement fund is just extra cash you wouldn't have received. This technique doesn't reduce the benefits either one of you will receive when you do start drawing based on your own earnings record.

It may sound fishy or like double dipping, but it's totally legal. After all, you paid into the system for many years and the government made the rules. All you're doing is following the rules.

By all means, don't try to receive benefits from your own earnings and from your spouse's earnings at the same time. This is called "deeming" and is not legal. Visit your local Social Security office and they can explain how to make this work. It's totally legal. You just have to ask for it.

Incidentally, if you want to know a lot more about Social Security and other income maximizing strategies, I highly recommend the book *Get What's Yours–The Secrets to Maxing Out Your Social Security* by Laurence J. Kotlikoff and Philip Moeller. You can find the book on Amazon.

Your eyes are probably glazed over by now, so let's move on to what you really want to know: how can you enjoy the RV life while living on your Social Security income?

Since the title of the book is *Secrets of RVing on Social Security,* I think it's reasonable for you to assume that, yes, it can be done. The rest of this book is dedicated to showing you how to do it and proving to you that it can be done and done in a way that's enjoyable and stress-free.

Bottom line: As was stated at the beginning of this chapter, the average person gets $1,341 a month from Social Security, but if you've gone through the steps outlined in this chapter, you should have a pretty good idea of exactly how much your Social Security income will be. Keep that number in mind as you go through the rest of this book, and let's see what we can do with that income. I think you'll be pleasantly surprised.

In later chapters, I'll also talk about ways to make additional money that can supplement your Social Security income while you're on the road.

Chapter 2

How Much will it Cost to Live the RV Lifestyle?

"I have found that there ain't no surer way to find out whether you like people or hate them than to travel with them."

~ Mark Twain

The short answer to how much it will cost to live full time in an RV is that it will cost the same as it does to live in a house or a condo—that is, it will cost whatever you have.

One big advantage of living the RV lifestyle is that you have a lot more control over your monthly expenses. When you live a traditional lifestyle, most of your expenses are fixed and there is not much you can do to change them, at least, not on a month-to-month basis.

If you have a big auto repair bill this month, you can't decide to rent a lower priced condo for a month or so or to live in a house with a lower mortgage payment for a while. But you can lower (or even eliminate your fixed expenses) for a month or so when you're living the RV lifestyle.

For example, you can totally eliminate campground fees by boondocking for a month or so. (Boondocking is camping where you don't pay any fees, but you don't have access to water, electric, and sewer.) You can eliminate gasoline expenses by not traveling for a while.

I'll talk more about boondocking in chapter 9. RVs are self-contained and can easily go two weeks or more without having to take on more water or dump the sewer. Your RV will likely have a generator and maybe solar power for electricity, so either way you will have electricity.

If you've gone through the steps in the previous chapter, you should know how much money you will have coming in from Social Security each month. Add to that any additional money you will have coming in (if any) for pensions, rental property, investments, etc.

If you haven't stopped to go through the steps to determine how much you will have coming in, let's work with the number, $1,341, since that's what the government says is the average Social Security payment received by a person who is drawing Social Security. Of course, if there are two people drawing Social Security, that will give you more money to work with. Later I will talk about ways you can earn a little extra money while enjoying the RV lifestyle and living on the road, but for now. . .

Can you live the RV lifestyle on $1,341 a month?

Below are actual monthly expenses of some RVers who live active, but frugal RVing lives. These numbers are provided by some RVers who keep detailed records of their travel expenses and reveal exactly how much they have spent to live and travel in their RVs.

Becky Schade at Interstellarorchard.com posted that in her first four months of traveling in 2012 she spent a total of $4,393.01. That comes to $1,098 a month—well under the $1,331 figure we are working with.

These four months included driving from South Carolina to Kansas and then from Kansas to Wisconsin. It only included paying campground fees for one of those four months because she was working at Amazon and received free camping in addition to a salary for three of those four months.

In 2013 her average was $1,275 a month and for 2014 she averaged $1,333 a month. These numbers cover everything, including $1,000 for repairs on her truck and camper in 2014.

Sue at RvSueAndCrew.net posted expenses for the first three months of 2015 as follows:

Jan. $1,129

Feb. $1,553

March $1,098

Average for the three months was $1,260 a month.

The numbers Sue posted include about $130 every month for pet food. Also, the February amount was higher than normal because it included $408 for medical expenses (dental work and eye glasses), plus a charge of $150 for Verizon overage on data usage.

As you can see, some months have extra or unexpected expenses. Sue boondocks most of the time, so she doesn't have camping fees. This saves her a lot of money. You can see all of her expenses itemized for each month since 2012 by visiting her website at rvsueandcrew.net

Olivia and Kyle's total expenses for a recent month came out to $1,422 and that included $724 for food. That's a lot of eating out. You can see a complete breakdown of their expenses at the link below:

http://drivinvibin.com/2016/03/13/the-cost-of-rv-living-our-february-expenses

Paul and Nina at wheelingit.us have been full-time RVers since 2010 and have kept good records of what they spend. You can see their breakdown of expenses and their comments about the cost of full-time RVing at the link below:

wheelingit.us/2011/02/24/the-costs-of-full-time-rving

Their expenses of $985 a month for fixed costs and $450 for variable costs give them a total of $1,435 a month for living expenses. That's a little over our target of $1,341, but there are some things in their fixed costs that you might not have.

Your expenses could be even less than shown in the previous examples

For example, in the case of Paul and Nina, there's $200 a month for pet fees shown in their living expenses. I like pets. If you have one or more pets, you're probably not going to get rid of them, but face the facts if you're on a tight budget: pets are expensive. And pets can have unexpected vet bills that can get very expensive. My brother and his wife had to have emergency surgery for their little dog recently because of a blocked bladder. That cost them $1,800 and then there were follow-up vet bills after the surgery.

Another place to cut expenses in the above budget is the $110 a month they're spending for storage. Eliminating this expense is simple—don't put stuff in storage. They also show an expense of $150 a month for Internet/phone. I don't spend this much. You can get by with a basic cell phone package, and there is free WiFi available at most campgrounds—not very fast and not always reliable, but it's free.

Of course, if you're running a business using the Internet, you may need to pay this much in order to have fast and reliable Internet service, but if you're being frugal, you can probably get an Internet/phone package that will fit your business needs for $100 or less.

Note that in all of the examples above (if you go to the websites and checkout the details of the expense totals quoted), you won't see any expenses shown for paying off any debt or credit cards and no payments on a car, truck, or RV. Starting off debt free with your credit cards and rig paid for makes living the RV lifestyle on a tight budget much more manageable. I will talk a lot more about buying a motorhome or camper with the cash you have available in a later chapter.

Also, in the above lists of RV living expenses, not many campground fees are shown. Many people living the RVing lifestyle on a tight budget do a lot of boondocking on BLM land (Bureau of Land Management), which is government owned land that you can camp on free of charge in most cases, or they workamp and get free camping. I'll go into more details on both of these techniques later, but, for now, just know that the options exist.

When RVers are traveling, many of them stop and spend the night in Walmart parking lots. Most Walmarts allow it and it's free and safe. Be sure to check with the manager and get permission. A few Walmarts don't allow RVs to park overnight, but most do.

The last two times I parked overnight at Walmart, there were 20+ RVs there one night and 30+ the other night. Of course, I bought groceries and supplies from Walmart while I was there. It's a win-win situation. RVers get free overnight camping and Walmart gets extra business. There's no requirement that you buy stuff while you're there, but most RVers do as a way of saying thank you to the store for letting them park overnight. You can also stay overnight for free at most Pilot and Flying J truck stops.

You will need an emergency fund

My advice to anyone living the RV lifestyle is to keep an emergency fund. Don't buy the most expensive RV you can afford. Keep a little money back for emergencies. Also, make sure that you are not spending every penny that's coming in each month. If you find yourself spending all the money that's coming in, by all means, find a way to do some workamping or other ways to make a little extra money each month, or find a way to cut back on your spending, so you can put away some money for an emergency.

Things happen when you're living on the road—just as they do when you're living a traditional lifestyle. Below is a list of expenses that could come up at any time, and you need to be prepared for them.

- Eye glasses.

- Dental work. (I broke a tooth yesterday. I'm sure that will be expensive and it's not covered by insurance.)

- Tires—you may have a blowout at any time and even if you don't, you will need to replace all of your tires every five to seven years. If you have three years left on your tires, start putting money aside now for a new set. Saving $50 a month for three years would give you $1,800 towards a set of tires when the time comes.

- If you have an accident, your insurance will probably cover it, but is there a deductible amount that you would be required to pay?

When unexpected expenses happen, if you have the funds to cover the expense, there's no big problem. You pay the money and then you take steps (as described above) to temporarily reduce your living expenses or make extra income for a month or so to replace the money in your emergency fund, and life goes on. It's when you have an unexpected expense and don't have the money to cover it that life gets complicated.

I know of several people who are mostly boondocking and living the RV lifestyle on $500 a month, but $1,000 or more a month makes life a lot more enjoyable.

Bottom line: The numbers and links provided in this chapter show you that it is possible to live on a typical Social Security monthly check. This is assuming that you are not paying off any debt and that you have the money to pay cash for your RV up front. If you're paying off any debt or plan to finance your RV, you may need additional sources of income to make ends meet—such as doing some workamping. Ways of supplementing your Social Security income are covered in chapter 10.

Chapter 3

What Would Life Be Like Living in an RV?

"Thanks to the interstate highway system, it is now possible to travel from coast to coast without seeing anything."

~ Charles Kuralt

Charles Kuralt's quote explains why I like to travel without using the Interstate unless I'm in a hurry to get somewhere—and I try not to be in a hurry. The most interesting things won't be found by driving down the Interstates.

For most RVers their goal when traveling is not to get somewhere, but to enjoy the journey. I was talking to a couple yesterday. They were headed from North Carolina to Wisconsin, and they felt they would have to rush because they had only a little over two weeks to get there. That's the mindset of RVers. They travel a short distance, stop for a few days, and then travel some more. They usually don't travel every day, and they don't get in a hurry.

What is it like to live the RV lifestyle is not an easy question to answer

People are always asking me what it's like to live full time in an RV. They want to picture themselves living the full-time RV lifestyle so they can decide if they would enjoy it and be happy.

Living in an RV is not like living in a conventional house, condo, or apartment. If you asked what it would be like to live in a mountain cabin by a lake, or live in a condo on the beach, or live in a retirement community in Florida, or live in a middle-class subdivision in Little Rock, or live on a farm in Kansas, that question would be a lot easier to answer. It would be easier to answer because in each of these situations, things are a lot more defined and stable.

I bet you could fairly easily describe what it's like to live the lifestyle you're living now—mainly because it's fairly routine. There's not much that changes. Many (maybe most) people like a stable, predictable lifestyle. You probably did for a long time, but now you're thinking about making a change or you wouldn't be looking into the feasibility of living the RV lifestyle.

The problem with trying to describe what it's like to live the RV lifestyle is that there are hundreds of different lifestyles that full-time RVers choose. And to make it even harder to explain, many of them change their lifestyle from month to month or even week to week. I know I do.

A "slice-of-life" or "snapshot" of RV life

This past January I spent my time in state and county parks up and down the East Coast of Florida. I stayed from St. Augustine to Vero Beach. I didn't go below Vero Beach because the rates in South Florida in the winter get higher the farther south you go. I liked being on the beaches during January when it was cold in the rest of the country.

Staying in Florida state parks runs about $18 to $24 a night and is a little over my budget, but I splurge sometimes to be near the beach. Of course, if you're 65 or older and have Florida as your domicile state (meaning you decide to be a resident of Florida, which I'll talk about in chapter 11), you can stay in Florida state parks for half-price. That really helps the budget.

In February I did some boondocking (which was free) and got my budget back in line. Yes, you can find places to boondock in Florida—just not on or near the beaches. I also stopped in Walmart parking lots the days I was traveling. This was also free. I like free. I'll talk a lot more about boondocking in chapter 9.

I spent March in one place. Staying in one place saves on gas, and the monthly rate at commercial campgrounds is about half-price compared to the weekly rate. I was on the Gulf Coast parked right next to the water, but it wasn't the beach. You can find monthly rates in Florida (even during the busy winter season) in the $350 to $450 range. Of course, it's even cheaper in the summer, but Florida in the summer is too hot for me.

By the way, to give you another "slice"'of the RV lifestyle, below is a link to a YouTube video showing the regular Sunday morning gospel music jam session at one of the RV parks where I stayed. You can see my white motorhome parked near the clubhouse as I pan the camera around towards the water.

Youtube.com/watch?v=5_9WUxtRwN4

In April, when it started getting warm/hot in Florida, I headed to the cooler North Carolina mountains for the summer months. Boone and Black Mountain, North Carolina, are two of my favorite areas in the mountains. I like hiking to waterfalls. High Falls in the Dupont State Park near Brevard, North Carolina, is one of my favorites. I hiked there recently with two other RVers I had met at a campground. You'll find that RVers like to get out and do things; they're an adventurous bunch.

Here is a picture of part of the falls. The falls are over 100 feet high, so I couldn't get all of the falls in the picture when I was up close—and I like to be up close to feel the mist.

Everything I have described here is what I call a "slice of life" or a "snapshot" of my different RVing experiences. Of course, this summer will be different and then next winter will be different from this past winter. That's why it's hard to describe exactly what it's like living the RV lifestyle. It changes all the time—and that's the beauty of it. It changes because I choose to make it change. I could choose to visit the same places, but I like to experience new places.

Next year I may decide to spend a major part of the summer months in the Rocky Mountains. There are a lot more free boondocking camping places in the western part of the US than there are in the eastern part. Every night that you can camp for free gives you that much more money in the budget for gas and traveling.

One of the things I enjoy about the RVing lifestyle is being able to hike in different and interesting places. I like being outside a lot and in touch with nature. The naturalist John Burroughs summed up my feelings in his quote below:

> *"I go to nature to be soothed and healed, and to have my senses put in order."*
>
> *~ John Burroughs*

What you'll learn sitting around a campfire at an RV park

If you want to get an idea of how diverse the different RVing lifestyles are, just sit around a campfire at a campground and listen to the conversations. You'll find that:

- Some people like to travel every few days.

- Some people like the large, comfortable rigs.

- Some people like the small motorhomes or campers that are easier to handle and easier to get into the out-of-the-way places.

- Some people like to travel solo and some travel with a spouse.

- Some people like to stay in one place for a season and some travel at least every week.

- Some people like to travel just a few miles a day and some like to make a lot of miles on travel days.

- Some people like to work part time at Amazon or work doing camp-hosting or other interesting jobs.

To make it even harder to describe what it's like to live full time in an RV, a lot of people do a mixture of these traveling lifestyles. They may spend three months in one campground in Florida or Arizona during the winter months and then travel a lot during the other months (sometimes staying in one place for a day or two and sometimes staying for a week or two). A lot of people like to boondock for several weeks on BLM (Bureau of Land Management) land. Some people like to boondock almost all the time.

You don't drive every day

The average RV is driven about 3,500 miles a year. That's less than 300 miles a month. That's why if you look at a 10-year-old RV, it will likely have about 30,000 to 40,000 miles on it.

Even if you have a goal to visit every state or to see every national park, go slowly the first year. Don't overdo the travel. The state and national parks will all be there next year, and the year after. They're not going anywhere. Slow down and have fun. Enjoy the journey.

How one RVer described the lifestyle

One full-time RVer told me recently that at his last high school reunion, someone said to him, "You're the happiest and most relaxed person here. What are you doing with your life that makes you so happy?" If you decide to embark on the full-time RVing lifestyle, someone might ask you that same question at your next reunion.

Bottom line: Living the RV lifestyle on your Social Security is whatever you want it to be (within your budget). And by mixing in some free boondocking days, some workamping, and some frugal living, you can have a lot of flexibility and enjoyment while still staying within your budget.

Chapter 4

RV Life—Pros, Cons and Things to Consider

"To succeed in life, you need two things: ignorance and confidence."

~ *Mark Twain*

If you're like I was when I started living the RV lifestyle, you probably have the "ignorance" part about RVing mastered. Now let's work on the confidence.

Personal note: Back when I was working on getting an instrument rating to go with my private pilot license, one time my instructor told me that I had more confidence than skill. That's not a good situation when you're coming in for a landing on a foggy, dark night and you can't see anything except the airplane's instruments. Now that I have my instrument rating and over 2,000 hours of flying time, hopefully I have the skill to go with the confidence I had back in my early days of flying.

When I started the RVing lifestyle, I had the ignorance for sure, but I also had the confidence that if other people could live this life, I could too. After three years of being on the road, I'm sure I still have a lot to learn, but I know a lot more than I did when I started.

One thing that gives you confidence is doing things. Because I've done it, I now know that I can. For example, I can drive my Class A rig through downtown Atlanta traffic during rush-hour; maneuver through the very narrow streets in historic downtown St. Augustine, Florida; drive up the narrow, winding, two-lane mountain road going to Boone, North Carolina; and I can back into tight camping spaces by myself after dark. These things don't scare me anymore—because I've done them and now know that I can do them.

Pros, cons, and things to consider when you're thinking about living full time in an RV

The Pros:

- Freedom. You can live where you want to and move with the seasons. You are not tied down. You can change your mind tonight and live somewhere else tomorrow night. You can go wherever whim and chance might take you.

- One of the things I like even more than going to different places is the freedom to know that I can go if I want to.

- If you change your mind about the RV lifestyle, you can sell an RV in a matter of days or weeks instead of the months or years it can take to sell a house.

- If you don't like your neighbors, you can move to another location in a matter of minutes.

- You can travel internationally and not have to still be paying living expenses back home while you're gone. Just put your RV in storage at $50 a month or so while you're gone. In fact, most RV insurance policies allow you to drop your liability insurance when you're not driving your RV and then reinstate the policy when you hit the road again.

- When I was between houses, condos and RVs, I spent six months living in Costa Rica. It was a fun and interesting experience. It was very inexpensive, but it wouldn't have been so inexpensive if I had been paying for rent (or a mortgage payment), electricity, cable TV, Internet, taxes, etc., back home. When you're living in an RV, you have the freedom to almost totally eliminate expenses back home while you travel abroad. Whether you ever do it or not doesn't matter. Just having the freedom to do it is a good feeling.

- Having everything I need handy is one thing I really like. I know where all of my tools are. I know where my books and my clothes are. Nothing is in storage or somewhere out in the garage or somewhere up in the attic. It's all right here.

- I like the idea of arranging my travels so that I can stop and see friends and family who live in different parts of the country.

The Cons:

I had a hard time finding things to list in this section because I like almost everything about RV living, but that's just me. Here are some things that may be considered cons for some people:

- You don't have as much privacy in campgrounds (sometimes you do, particularly in state parks, but not always).

- Sometimes there are noises like barking dogs, RVs pulling in and out, traffic from busy highways, or trains on nearby railroad tracks.

- You won't have your "back-home" friends nearby to enjoy and spend time with.

- Your regular doctors may not be close by.

- Most RVs have a one-butt kitchen.

- In a conventional home the water, electricity, WiFi, and TV signal just come out of the holes in the walls that they're supposed to and the poop disappears to I don't know or care where. I set the trash bags outside and they disappear. I don't worry about any of those things. In the RV I have to worry about all of these things to make sure that they don't run out or run over. If either one of these things happens, it's a big problem—so I've heard, Yeah, right.

- In 10 minutes flat, the whole place can become trashed. Of course, in 15 minutes I can vacuum, wipe everything down, pick things up, clean the bathroom, and have the place back in order.

Other Things to Consider

- If you are a couple, do you both really want this adventure?

- Do you both have hobbies, interests or things you really like to do that don't involve the other person—reading, writing, knitting, crafts, computers, golf, fishing, hiking, painting, etc.?

- Do you have things or people "back home" that you need to look after or take care of—rental property, aging parents, etc.?

- Headsets or ear buds are mandatory when two people are living in an RV.

- How comfortable are you and your spouse being together 24/7? The little things that annoy you about your spouse can get magnified when you're together 24/7 in a small space. Most people need a little time apart. There are ways to do this while living in an RV, but give it some consideration. Be sure to schedule some "me" time. Of course, the work you will be doing could give you some away time—unless you're both making your income by doing computer work.

- Just as in a stick and brick home (RVer jargon), there will be unexpected maintenance expenses from time to time. Allow for these expenses in your budget.

- If you act like a tourist and want to eat out a lot and see and do things like a tourist, you will end up spending money like a tourist. To keep your expenses low, you have to remember that you're not on vacation.

- Life in an RV can be much less expensive than a traditional lifestyle—but you have to learn a few secrets and techniques that I cover in later chapters. One of the big ways RV life can be substantially less expensive (than life in a stick and brick home) is the option not to travel for a month, or so, and, instead, stay in a campground where you can get free camping in exchange for volunteer work. Then, your living expenses will be almost nothing—except food, insurance, etc. You also have the option of boondocking part of the time. When living the RV lifestyle, you will also save a lot of money by not buying things you don't need. Going shopping will no longer be considered a form of entertainment. There's no place to put things you don't really need.

What do I miss about my old lifestyle?

A lot of non-RVers ask me this question, but I can't think of much I miss about my previous lifestyle. I think more about what I would miss if I gave up my RV lifestyle. Here are some of the things I would miss if I gave up living in my RV:

- Being free to travel and see the country

- Going to music festivals and rallies

- Enjoying 75 and 80 degree January and February days

- Hour-long coffee times with friends

- Spending time with wonderful, like-minded people

- Sunrises and sunsets over water

- Never having to deal with snow and cold weather

- Always having friends nearby to have a glass of wine with from time to time without having to take more than a few steps

- Sitting around a campfire with interesting friends

- Being able to explore charming little towns

- Always being near new and interesting hiking trails

In other words, total freedom.

When I talk to other RVers, I find out that, for most of them, their biggest regret is that they didn't embark on this lifestyle sooner.

Make your decision

This book, along with the links, references and other books I recommend, will give you the information you need to make your decision—but you have to make the decision.

In one of my marketing classes at Harvard Business School, a professor asked a student what he would do in the case being studied. The student said that he would go out and get more information. That was the wrong answer.

The professor said, "Every decision you make for the rest of your life will be made with incomplete information." He said, "Do a reasonable amount of research and investigation and then make a decision. If it's wrong, you can change it." He said that businesses lose more money by not making a decision than they ever lose by making a wrong decision.

I think that concept applies to personal decisions, too.

What if you change your mind about RVing?

Full-time RVing is not for everyone. Not everyone is cut out for this lifestyle, individually or as a couple.

Selling an RV can be done fairly easily in a matter of a week or two, or a month or two at the most. In fact, you can list your RV on eBay and sell it in three days—and at a fair price.

You are not locked in. You can change your lifestyle in a heartbeat. And if you do your homework and find a great deal (and do a good job of negotiating) when you buy your RV, you can likely sell it for more than you paid for it.

Bottom line: Do a reasonable amount of research, soul-searching and fact-finding, and then make your decision. You will never have all of the information, but, remember, when you're living the RV lifestyle, it's easy to change your mind, sell your RV, and live a different lifestyle.

Keep reading and then make your decision.

Chapter 5

How to Get Rid of your Stuff

"A house is just a place to keep your stuff while you go out and get more stuff."

~ George Carlin

You can't hit the road until you get rid of your stuff, so let's stop ignoring the elephant in the room and face the fact that you have to part with a lot of stuff if you want to live the full-time RV lifestyle.

I don't know how many times I've heard someone say, "I could never live in an RV—I have too much stuff." If this describes your thinking, remember the stuff doesn't own you. You own the stuff.

People say this with the same conviction they would say that one leg is longer than the other one. They act as though they were born that way and that there is nothing they can do about it.

If you say, "I choose to have all of this stuff," then you own the situation or problem. It's easier to deal with when you look at it that way.

When you get rid of the things that clutter your house, it also un-clutters your mind. Try it and you will see.

The phrase, *"Digging through my closet"* no longer applies.

One woman's approach to getting rid of stuff

There's a #1 bestselling book that came out in October 2014 that might help you get rid of your stuff. The book is . . .

The Life-Changing Magic of Tidying Up: The Japanese Art of Decluttering and Organizing by Marie Kondo.

You can find the book on Amazon. It's not about moving into an RV, but I think you will find it helpful if you're having trouble getting rid of your stuff.

In a nutshell, these are the four main pieces of advice I got out of her book:

1. Pick up each item and ask yourself if it sparks joy. In other words, does it make you happy? If not get rid of it.

2. Sort by category, not location. Don't start with the bedrooms, and then the study, and then the kitchen, etc., do all of your clothes and then all your books, and so on.

3. Tidy each category all at one time. Don't do a little bit today and more tomorrow. You'll never get finished.

Go through all of your clothes at one time and then all of your books at one time.

4. Don't keep gifts just because you would feel guilty if you threw them away. After you have experienced the joy of the gift-giving moment, you can donate the gift without feeling guilty. The gift has served its purpose.

There are a lot of other good points in the book and her writing style makes it a fun read. For example, she says that socks need to be stored unfolded so they can relax. She said, "They take a brutal beating in their daily work, trapped between your foot and your shoe. The time they spend in your drawer is their only chance to rest." Makes sense to me.

I took a different approach to getting rid of stuff

Kondo's techniques for tidying up and getting rid of stuff work for a lot of people, but being an engineer, I took a more logical approach to getting rid of my stuff. Below is the approach I used. Perhaps, if you're having trouble getting rid of your stuff, you could use a combination of the two techniques.

The approach that worked for me was to start with the concept that all my stuff could be classified into one of four categories: A, B, C, and D.

Category A: Things you really are going to use and take with you in your RV—and remember a Class A motorhome can hold a lot of stuff.

Category B: These are the things that you can sell—your dining room table and chairs, the sofa you bought two years ago, your riding lawnmower. In fact, you can sell almost everything and it doesn't take long to do it.

Craigslist is a great way to sell larger items. If you price the items right and include pictures, they will usually sell within a week. If an item doesn't sell within a week, lower the price by at least a third and list it again. Be sure to list a phone number on which you can be reached most of the time.

When someone is ready to buy something, if they can't get you on the phone, they will call another person selling essentially the same type of item you're offering. I have sold a lot of items using craigslist. The system works great. You get a fair price and you get it sold quickly.

For smaller items, you can use eBay. For both craigslist and eBay, be sure to show several good quality pictures. Pictures make items sell in a hurry. With eBay, you can set a reserve price, or you can just auction it off and take what you get. After all, usually, whatever it sells for is what it's worth and that's what you wanted to do in the first place—sell the item for whatever it's worth.

I like to run an eBay auction for three days and start the bidding at $1. That gets a lot of people bidding. You can also offer a "Buy it Now" option with eBay. A lot of people don't want to wait. They want to buy your item and be done with it.

One word of caution, don't accept a cashier's check when selling something on craigslist. Cashier's checks are easy to counterfeit. Even after they have cleared, they can still be charged back to you. Someone wanting to pay with a cashier's check is a common craigslist scam technique. Don't fall for it. Take cash only.

Category C: These are the things that you put in a garage sale one Saturday and then take what doesn't sell to Goodwill. This way, at the end of the day, everything in this category is gone.

Basically, Category C items are things that you could buy at Goodwill for almost nothing IF you ever really needed them. In this category would be tools, old furniture, clothes, shoes, items you bought at garage sales because they were such bargains, all the extra dishes and cookware that you might use if you ever had 30 people come to visit, all of the extra towels and linens—the list goes on. Get rid of these things in a hurry.

Category D: This category is for sentimental things. A few of these things you can take with you—but very few. Pictures and photo albums can all be scanned and put on a thumb drive. If you don't know how to do this, there are businesses that offer this service at a very low price.

There's Grandma's sewing machine, Great-Grandma's lamp, the afghan that Aunt Sarah made for you, etc. Most people think that things on this list are the hardest to get rid of. But, in fact, these items can be the easiest to get rid of if you follow the procedure described below.

How to get rid of sentimental things

First of all, decide who you want to have each of these things when you're dead and gone. (I know, you consider that to be a long way off, but think about it this way anyway.) Then give the items to that person now. If they won't take the things now, you know what will happen to them as soon as you're gone. They will give them to Goodwill, sell them in a garage sale or just throw them away. If you have a few items that you want your grandchildren to have when they're grown (and you don't trust your children to keep the items for them), you can put these items in storage, but think about how expensive five or ten years of storage will be before you do this.

I know that it's hard to accept the fact that a lot of things you cherish will not even be considered worth keeping by other people when you're gone. That's just the facts. Don't blame your children or relatives. It's not their responsibility or duty to like or value the same things you like.

Remember, when you give someone something, it now belongs to them. Be sure to tell them this. If they want to sell it in a garage sale, that's fine with you. Of course, that's probably not the way you feel, but there's no need to lay a guilt trip on them and insist that they keep the item and cherish it. Even if they do keep it for a while, it may get thrown away later.

A lot of the things you will be giving people will be things that they will love and really enjoy having. By giving them the items now, you will get to see them enjoy these things and you'll know the items went to the people you wanted to have them.

Don't put things in storage

By all means don't just put things in storage—at least, not more than will fit in the smallest storage unit they make, and not without setting a date to determine whether you're continuing as a full-time RVer.

If you do put things in a storage unit, consider getting rid of even those things a year from now. Some people have found it easier to get rid of sentimental things in a two step process like this, but don't let it drag out into years and still have your belongings in storage.

In other words, put those things you think you just can't part with in storage for one year. At the end of a year decide if your future is full-time RVing. If so, give everything that's in storage to your relatives. If they don't want the items, sell them. If something doesn't sell, give it to Goodwill or throw it away.

I know of one couple who put things into a storage unit and didn't even see any of the things for seven years before they finally decided to go back and empty out the storage unit. The items in their storage unit were not sentimental things, it was just stuff.

I also know a woman who has a very large storage unit that she pays $200 a month for and she has had it for over 5 years. That's over $12,000 she has paid and I wouldn't give $200 for everything in her storage unit. Most of it's not even sentimental items, it's just things that she thinks she might need someday. Don't fall into this trap. Even $50 a month for five years is still $3,000 and $3,000 will buy a lot of stuff.

If you put a big, new storage building behind your house, how long do you think it would be before it would be full? Most of us tend to store stuff until all available space is filled.

Even with the limited storage space in my motorhome, I find from time to time that I have accumulated a lot of stuff—things like the cardboard box that my backup camera came in (I thought I might want to return it sometime), and the power supply for the electric razor that quit working. I threw the razor away, but I still have the power supply. Who knows? I might need it for something sometime. I think we are all pack rats by nature, but we can change.

It will feel like a tremendous burden is lifted from your shoulders when you have gotten rid of all of the stuff you didn't really need.

One thing that helps in getting rid of things is to set a date by which everything has to be gone. For a storage unit that can be easy, just say, "I'm not going to pay another month's rent. Everything has to be out by the 31st."

Bottom line: You have all of this stuff because you choose to have it. Therefore, you can choose to get rid of it. You may not believe it now, but it's such a big relief when you get rid of all of the stuff that you've been hanging on to for years.

I know one couple who made a picture of their empty storage unit and then threw a party and invited their friends to help them celebrate the big occasion. It was a fun time.

Plan your party now to celebrate your freedom from STUFF!

Chapter 6

What Kind of RV to Get?

"The traveler sees what he sees. The tourist sees what he has come to see."

~ *G. K. Chesterton*

In one way deciding what type of RV you should get is hard, but looking at it another way, it may be a fairly easy task. Let me explain.

First, the reason it could be considered hard to make a decision on what type of RV you should buy is because there are so many choices. There are motorhomes, camper/trailers, fifth-wheel rigs, and of course, all of these come in a lot of different sizes and price ranges.

To make matters worse, you probably don't have a clear idea about how you will be living and traveling when you start your new RVing lifestyle, so that makes it even more difficult to make the right decision about what type of RV to choose.

But, here's some good news. The reason it may not be a be problem after all is that over half of the people who are living full time in their RV sell their first RV and get a different one within two years.

In other words, your first RV is probably not the one you will keep for very long, so you don't have to select the perfect RV. The only thing that's important is that you get a good deal on your first RV, so you can sell it in a year or so and get your money out of it and, hopefully, even make a small profit. That's easier to do than you might think. The reason this is possible is because there are so many real bargains out there when it comes to buying an RV—you just have to do the research and legwork and find them. I'll talk more about that later.

As stated before, it's a fact that most RVers will have a different rig after two years of RVing than they start out with. The main reason this happens is because most new RVers don't know what kind of rig will be best for their lifestyle. How could you really know until you've been on the road for a while?

Would you be better off with a motorhome and, if so, would a Class A, Class C, or Class B work better? Or maybe a fifth-wheel and truck would be better. How about a camper/trailer? And even if they knew for sure which would work best for them, what size should they get? Bigger is not always better. I've met a lot of RVers who have sold their rigs and bought smaller ones.

It's not only that they don't know much about RVs, they also may not know much about what they will be doing, how much they will be traveling, and how long they will be staying in one place. Even if they do think they know these things, their plans may change.

Knowing all of this, it's a good idea for new RVers to get a good deal when they buy their first RV. By a good deal, I mean they should try real hard to buy an RV that they can sell within a year or two and not lose any money on the deal—and maybe even make a profit.

Making a profit is easier to do than you might think. As my father said, you make your profit when you buy, not when you sell. When you sell something, you can expect to get about what it's worth. You might luck up and sell something for more than it's really worth, but don't plan on it. But it is possible to buy an RV for less than it's worth—if you do your homework. I have been offered more for my motorhome than I paid for it, but I'm not interesting in selling it right now.

Don't buy a new RV as your first RV. You will lose your shirt if you try to sell a new RV a few years after you buy it. New RVs depreciate much faster than new cars.

Stack the deck in your favor and do the work it takes to get a really good deal on your first RV—and remember, there are a lot of great deals out there.

First, let's take a look at the pros and cons of the different types of motorhomes

There are five basic types of motorhomes: Class A, Class B, Class B+, Class C, and then there are conversion buses. If you're wondering how the different classes of motorhomes got their names, I'll explain. The Class C motorhomes were called a Class C because they were built on a chassis. Then the larger and fancier motorhomes came on the market and, naturally, they were called Class A. Much later the smaller motorhomes (a little bigger than a van) came along and, for marketing purposes, they didn't want to call them a Class D because that would imply that they were inferior, so they went with what was left—the Class B. When they started making the Class B motorhomes a little bigger (and some with slides), naturally, they called these Class B+. And now you know—there is a little rhyme and reason to how motorhomes got their names, but not much.

One other fact about motorhomes is that most people who live full time in a motorhome find that they need to tow a car, and this adds to the expense.

There are also vans and truck campers, but I'll leave these out of the discussion because I don't consider them to be realistic for full-time RVing—although some people do find them acceptable.

Class A motorhomes

These are the large motorhomes that look like a Greyhound bus with a large front windshield. They range in length from about 25 feet to about 48 feet. They are great for full-time RVing because of all of the room and also because they have a lot of storage under the coach. This space is appropriately called the basement since it's under the main living quarters. New Class A motorhomes can be expensive, but you can find some real bargains in used ones—mainly because people think they are hard to drive and think they get poor gas mileage. The truth is that, with a little prac-tice (you can do the practice in a parking lot), you'll likely find that driving a Class A motorhome is easier than you thought and a lot of fun. I love the view from that big, 8-foot wide and 4-foot high windshield. A Class A motorhome is more aerodynamic than a Class C and, therefore, gets only about one mile per gallon less than a large Class C motorhome. I have a 34-foot Class A motorhome and I get eight mpg pulling a car. Most of the Class A motorhomes manufactured after about 2000 have one or more slides. This makes the inside feel much larger.

Class C motorhomes

These are the motorhomes that have the extension over the cab. They basically look like a U-Haul™ moving truck. They are great for vacations and weekend family trips. Some of them can be as large as the smaller Class A motorhomes, but they are not as well suited to full-time living because they don't have much storage. I have friends who live full time in Class C motorhomes. A Class C is easier to drive, back, and park, and gets about one mpg better gas mileage than a Class A. Some of the larger Class C motorhomes have slides, but most don't.

Class B motorhomes

These are the smaller motorhomes that are a little larger than a van. They are taller so you can stand up inside them (if you're not over six feet or so tall). They get 13 to 15 mpg, and if you get the more expensive Mercedes diesel engine, you can expect to get about 20 mpg or maybe even a little better. They're easy to drive. In fact, they drive about like an SUV. And you can park them in a regular parking place. Because of these facts, a lot of people want them and, therefore, that runs the price of used ones up. They don't have much storage at all. I have a friend who has a Class B and he loves it, but he doesn't live in it full time and just uses it for when he wants to get away for a week or so. In fact, he uses it as a second car and drives it to the store or mall from time to time. Because of their high price and small space, I wouldn't recommend a Class B motorhome for full-time living, and especially not for more than one person—but I do know people who travel and live full time in their Class B motorhomes and they love it. Because of the good gas mileage, they are good for one person who wants to do a lot of traveling from time to time. Now that I've told you that a Class B motorhome is not a good choice for full-time RVing, below is link to a web page where Vanessa Fox tells about living in her Class B motorhome and how much she likes it.

GirlMeetsRoad.com/inside-roadtrek-170-popular-non-cartoon-transformer

Class B+ motorhomes

A Class B+ motorhome is, as you might expect, a little larger and fancier than a Class B. It's wider, longer, has a larger bathroom, and more storage. Some Class B+ models have a slide to provide even more room. The only problem with a Class B+ is that, since it seems to have everything a lot of people want (such as being easy to drive and getting good gas mileage), they are in high demand. This makes them expensive, but there are some bargains to be found in the older models if you do enough searching.

Bus Conversion

At first thought, you might think that converting a bus into a motorhome would be a way to save a lot of money. Whether it's a Greyhound type of bus or a school bus, don't go this route to save money. I have several friends who have converted buses and they love them. The good thing about converted buses is that they will run forever and they are unique and personalized. I think of them like owning a pet. You love it, and you would never think of getting rid of it, but you didn't buy it to save money. Later, when you know more about RVs and what you like and don't like, going the converted bus route might be a project that you would enjoy, but don't go that route now.

All of this just goes to show that there is no one right answer when it comes to choosing the perfect RV for living the full-time RV lifestyle. Do your homework and remember that your first RV will probably not be the one you end up living in long term.

Now let's take a look at the non-motorized RVs—travel trailers and fifth-wheel rigs

Going with a travel trailer or fifth-wheel rig is a good choice for a lot of people. I have a lot of friends who go this route and love their rigs. You have to have a truck to pull them, but then you don't need to pull a toad. They are more trouble to set up and take down, but you get a lot of room for the money. They are particularly nice if you plan to stay in one place a lot and not travel very often.

Travel Trailers (also called campers)
These come in a wide range of sizes—from the small 15-foot Casitas to very large models with slides and a lot of living space. There are many lightweight models on the market now that can be towed with smaller vehicles. Travel trailers are good for living full time if you're not going to be traveling a lot. It takes longer to get them hooked up and on the road than it does a motorhome. They are a lot less expensive than a motorhome, but, of course, you have to have a truck or SUV to pull them. They don't have a lot of storage space, but

you do have the back of the truck or SUV for storage. You can get a lot of living space for very little money in a travel trailer. A lot of people find them ideal when they want to live in them for part of the year (like winters in Florida or New Mexico) and then store them for $50 a month during the summers. A lot of campsites offer this service and will store your travel trailer and then have it set up when you arrive. This way, you don't even need a truck to tow it, but that's probably not the lifestyle you're considering. My guess is that you want to do some traveling, at least for now.

Fifth-wheel campers

These are great for full-time living. They are the largest size of travel trailers. They have a fair amount of storage, but not as much as a Class A motorhome. The master bedroom is in the front, and that leaves the back for another bedroom or a large living area with a big picture window. Most of them have slides. It takes a big truck with a special hitch in the bed to pull a fifth-wheel camper. This adds to the expense of the total rig. A lot of full-timers go with a fifth-wheel rig. If you're on a tight budget, a fifth-wheel camper plus a big truck is probably not the best way to go. The combination can get expensive.

Which rig is right for you?

The first step in selecting the best rig for you is to give a lot of thought to what you want to do and how you want to live when you become an RVer. Knowing this will help you know what kind of rig would be best for you. Who knows? Maybe you will get lucky and the first RV you buy will turn out to be exactly the perfect RV for you. When I say, "get lucky," that's probably the best way to describe it. There's not much of a chance that you will know enough about RVs, or enough about your needs or wants, to make a perfect buying decision when you buy your first RV.

In my case, I think I got lucky. I've had my motorhome three years and I'm very happy with it. I think I got just the right RV for me, but not because I knew exactly what kind of RV would be right for me. I'm convinced that I just got lucky. I did my homework and did some research, but I didn't have all of the answers—in fact, I don't even think I knew all of the questions. That's why I say I got lucky.

Keep in mind that the more research you do and the more homework you do, the luckier you're likely to get, so let's get started.

Do your research, looking, and soul-searching
Earlier in this chapter I gave you a general overview of the different kinds of RVs and the pros and cons of each type. Look over these descriptions again and then take an afternoon and go visit some RV dealerships where they have several RVs of all types for you to look at. Leave your checkbook at home. It's easy to fall in love with a particular RV, and it's also easy to fall in love with some of the new, fancy rigs. And the salesman will be all too happy to show you how you can own it with very low monthly payments. Don't fall for this. You have a lot more homework to do before you're ready to make a decision.

Walk through several of each of the different types of RVs. See how they feel. Look at floor plans and picture yourself living full time in each of the rigs. Don't worry too much about price. Right now your goal is to decide (well, not really decide yet, but get a gut feel about) whether you would like a Class A motorhome, a Class C, or a Class B. Then compare those to the fifth-wheel rigs and the travel trailers. Visit more than one dealership, and then go home and think about it. Talk to your spouse.

Then, as the shampoo bottle says, "lather, rinse, and repeat." In other words, on another day, go to a different RV dealership (maybe even in a different town), and do the same thing again. By the way, since most dealers keep their new and used RVs unlocked, you don't even need to go find a salesman to show you the rigs. Just start walking through them. Of course, don't be surprised if a salesperson shows up shortly to see if he can help you.

Be sure to consider how you're going to be using your rig. Are you going to be spending the summers in one area and the winters in another area and not doing much traveling in between? Or are you going to be doing a lot of traveling and staying for a week or a month in one area and then be off to somewhere else? How much you will be traveling will have a lot to do with which rig would be best for you.

It's hard to get unbiased information about RVs by asking other owners

The reason you can't ask different RV owners what kind of RV you should get is because almost everyone likes the kind they have. If they didn't, they would sell it and buy another type. That's one of the advantages of living in an RV compared to a stick and brick house or condo. You can sell an RV in a matter of days or weeks and get your money out of it. It's like selling a car. Put it on craigslist or eBay and you can get a fair price in a matter of days.

Bottom line: Any of the many different types and sizes of RVs can and are being used for full-time living. They all have their advantages and disadvantages. In my opinion, your best option for full-time RVing is to get one of the older

Class A or Class C motorhomes. If you're not going to be traveling much, a travel trailer might be a good choice. I wouldn't recommend a fifth-wheel rig (and the big truck it takes to pull it) if you're on a tight budget. They're nice and have a lot of room, but the rig and truck together can get expensive. If you're going to be traveling solo and doing a lot of traveling, you might consider a Class B motorhome, but those are more expensive, so they're probably not a good choice if you're on a tight budget.

Chapter 7

Cost of an RV and How to Find the Best Deals

"Live your life so you can say, 'when I grow up I want to be just like me.'"

~ unknown

Now that you have a pretty good idea about what kind of RV will work best for you and your planned lifestyle, let's talk about how to go about finding that type of RV and at a good price.

First of all, look at your budget. I highly recommend that you only buy an RV that you can afford to pay cash for and don't spend all of your cash. Save some money for repairs and some for an emergency fund. By all means, don't use the cash you have as a down payment on a higher priced rig and then have payments to meet each month—unless you're sure you will have a source of income that will allow you to make those monthly payments.

After a year or so when you know more about what type of RV would be best for you, if you can afford it and you want a newer and more expensive rig, that's the time to buy it, but not now.

Is it possible to get a really low-cost RV?

Yes it is. For example, Brett bought a 1985 Coachman Class C motorhome recently for $800 and hit the road. He drove it 1,000 miles on his first trip and everything worked fine. Below is a link to a video of him describing his $800 motorhome.

Youtube.com/watch?v=T_EoN9AkRek

Maybe he got lucky and found this bargain or maybe there are things wrong with the motorhome that he doesn't know about yet, but he has lived in it for over a year now with no problems. Either way, don't expect to find an RV for $800 that's livable and functional, but obviously it can be done.

I know two people who bought used motorhomes that sold originally for over $300,000, and they each got their rigs for less than $30,000. In other words, they are living in what was a top of the line motorhome just a few years ago, and they paid less than 10 cents on the dollar.

Here's another example of living in a low-cost motorhome. Pippi Peterson bought a 23-year-old large Class A motorhome and has fixed it up (new hardwood flooring, repaired the water heater, fixed leaks, redecorated, etc.) and now she has a very nice and dependable home. She said her remodeling costs were only $80 for materials (that was before she replaced the flooring), and she did most of the work herself as you can see in her videos.

She didn't say what she paid for her motorhome, but considering, it's 23 years old, I'm sure she got it for a song. (The going retail rate for this rig from a dealer would be about $7,000, but if you get it from an individual you might expect to get it for less than that.)

Below is a link to a YouTube video showing her rig.

Youtube.com/watch?v=X1EIdQN5rq0

By searching and negotiating, there are a lot of functional motorhomes that you can get for under $5,000. If your budget will allow you to go to the $10,000 to $25,000 range, you can get a really nice motorhome.

RVs in this price range won't be the newer models and more than likely will need some work done to them. If they don't need any work done on them immediately, plan on it down the road.

Keep some money in your budget for fixing things

There will almost always be a few things that will need to be fixed. One thing that a lot of used motorhomes need is new tires. A set of new tires will cost you about $2,000 to $2,500.

Be sure to check the date code on the tires of any RV you're considering. Tires are only good for five to seven years. (After five to seven years, tires will dry rot and start to crack and become dangerous to drive on, no matter how much tread is left.)

Look for the 4-digit date code on the tires (sometimes it's on the inside under the RV). It's the last four digits in the series of numbers and letters that start with "DOT", as shown in the photo below. The first two digits are the week and the second two are the year the tire was manufactured. The tire in the photo below was made in the 3rd week of 2013.

I recommend using a moisture meter when looking at a used RV. Below is a link to the one I recommended on Amazon:

http://www.amazon.com/gp/product/B00275F5O2

Two things to keep in mind when allocating money for repairs

1. If the inside of an RV you're looking at hasn't been taken care of, it's a good bet that the engine, brakes, belts, generator, etc. haven't been taken care of or serviced regularly either.

2. If the RV has been sitting for a while and has not been driven in a year or more, it will probably need some general (and maybe expensive) service. It could need belts, batteries, tires, brakes, etc. Of course, a camper that has been sitting unused will not need as much

work as a motorhome, but more than likely, it will still need some work to make it road-worthy.

How to find the actual prices that RVs recently sold for

Knowing what RVs like the one you're considering buying actually sold for recently will help you decide if that RV is within the price range you can afford.

Below is a link to a website that shows what RVs have recently sold for. I would consider these prices to be basically, more or less, retail prices. You should be able to buy a rig at a better price than what's shown on this website.

Pplmotorhomes.com/sold/soldmenu.htm

Another way to get an idea of what RVs are selling for is to check out eBay. Be sure to look at the "Completed listings" to see what RVs actually sold for. Sometimes the starting bid or the reserve price is way out of line and the RV will not sell.

To view the "Completed listings" and see the actual price RVs sold for, log into your eBay account and then in the top right corner of your screen, in small print (just to the right of the big blue "Search" box), you will see the word, "Advanced". Click on this link and then enter the keyword, "motorhome". Scroll down and click on the "Completed listings" box. Below that, enter a price range or at least enter a minimum price. If you don't enter a minimum price, you will see 20,000 items including mirrors, clocks, headlights, and everything that has the word "motorhome" in the listing.

Then click on the blue "Search" box. This will take you to the list of completed auctions. The prices shown in green are the ones that sold. The prices shown in red are the ones that didn't sell because their reserve price was higher than the highest bid or else they didn't get a bid because their starting bid was too high.

I think you will be pleasantly surprised at how little some of these motorhomes sell for.

Another way to compare RV prices (and find bargains) is to search craigslist.org in areas other than just in or near your city. You can use the Search Tempest website at the link below. The program will search for the type of RV you enter into the search box and search within the number of miles from your zip code that you select.

Searchtempest.com

You can also search by keyword and price. For example, if you wanted to find all of the motorhomes priced at $10,000 and below that are within 400 miles of your zip code (or another zip code), you can do that at this site.

How to handle the gap in price between what you want and what you can afford

Now that you have a general idea about what kind of RV you can get for what price, and you have an idea of what kind of RV you like and will fit your lifestyle, the next step is to look at your budget again. More than likely you will find that there's a gap between what you want and what you can afford.

This is sometimes called having champagne taste and beer money.

Don't give up. You may be able to find the RV that fits your needs for 20% to 40% less than the fair market retail value.

Don't be afraid to make a lowball offer. Sometimes you can get an RV for 50% less than the asking price. Knowing these two facts should put a lot more RVs back into your budget.

There are three ways to handle the problem of wanting a higher priced RV than your budget will allow.

1. The best way to handle the problem is to do more homework, legwork, and negotiating to find a real bargain. There are bargains out there. The old saying that you get what you pay for is not always true when it comes to RVs. You can get ripped off and pay way too much, but you can also end up with a great deal on your RV and pay way less than the market value. Don't ignore RV dealers. They usually have their used RVs set at a high retail price, but they will negotiate big time. I know of one case where a dealer sold a used RV for less than half of what he was asking for it. Don't be afraid to make a very lowball offer. If you have the cash and are ready to buy today, dealers will make some pretty good concessions, particularly on older RVs that have been on their lot for a while.

2. Another way to handle the problem is to change your wants. This is not such a bad option as you might think. The price of the RV you end up with will not have much to do with how happy you are living the RV lifestyle. I see people all the time who have very expensive rigs, and they don't seem nearly as happy as the people who have low priced rigs that they have customized, decorated, and turned into RVs with character. Go back and look at some of the lower priced RVs and think about what you can do with them to make them feel like home. And keep in mind that you can always sell the RV you start out with (maybe even

at a profit) and then buy a different one after you've been on the road for a while and know what you really want.

3. As a last resort, you could use the money you have and finance part of the purchase price of your RV. Keep in mind that financing older and lower priced RVs can be a problem. Only go this route if you have a source of income that will cover the monthly payments. That's usually hard to do on just a Social Security check, but if you will be working part of the time to bring in some extra money, it could work. I will talk about ways to make extra money while living the RV lifestyle in chapter 10.

The nitty-gritty of how to buy an RV at a bargain price

To get an RV at a bargain price, you need to find a seller who wants to get rid of his RV and doesn't really know the value or doesn't know how to present it and sell it for top dollar, or you have to find a seller who wants to sell his RV immediately for whatever reason. Maybe a dealer needs to get his monthly sales numbers up or maybe an individual needs the money or just wants to get rid of the RV.

In many cases, these RV owners don't take the time to shoot good pictures when they list their RVs, or they don't take very many pictures, and in a lot of cases they don't do a good job of describing their RV.

The more searching and looking you do, the better the deal you are likely to find. When you're doing your searching, be sure to make notes, and take pictures. If not, it won't take long before all the RVs you've looked at will run together in your head.

I like the idea of putting the information in a spreadsheet. You don't have to use a computer. You can just make a chart and list the brand, model, year, asking price, notes about condition, location, etc. This will make your selection process a lot more logical, and in the end you will feel like everything was considered.

Your final decision will be based on emotion and logic. You want to end up with an RV that your gut feel says is the right one for you, but you also want to feel that you made a logical decision in selecting your RV. Here's how to make all of this happen.

First start your search by looking in the right places
In addition to checking craigslist and local RV dealers in your area, keep in mind that you can find some good bargains outside of your area. Check in Florida, Arizona, Texas, and New Mexico. A lot of people go there to retire or they live there as snowbirds during the winter months, and then when they decide to stop RVing, they put their RVs up for sale. There are some real bargains to be found in these areas if you're diligent.

Be sure to check craigslist ads in these areas. When a snowbird decides to retire from the RV lifestyle, there's a good chance that their RV is in one of these states. The market is flooded in those areas, so the prices are lower. On the other hand, California, Oregon, and Washington are not good areas to find bargains. RVs sell for a lot more on the West Coast.

Even if you don't buy in any of the above locations, you can use the prices you find in these areas to help you negotiate the seller you're dealing with down to a lower price in many cases.

The second step is to negotiate your best price

One of the main reasons you want to negotiate a good deal when you buy your first RV is that, as we've discussed previously, there's a very good chance that you will be selling the first RV you purchase within one to two years. That's because it's hard to know exactly what kind of RV will be best for you and your lifestyle until you've been on the road for a while.

With that in mind, you want to buy your first RV at a price that will allow you to sell it within a year or so and hopefully make a small profit—or, at least, sell it and not lose much.

The key to selling your RV and making a profit is that you have to buy it at the right price—in other words, buy it at less than it's worth. There are bargains out there and, as a buyer with cash, patience, and the ability to negotiate, you can find an RV that's right for you and at a great price.

RV prices are usually more negotiable than car prices, so keep this fact in mind when you hear the initial asking price.

Some people don't like to negotiate, but in the RV market almost all prices are negotiable and not just a little bit, but a lot. You can save a lot of money by doing just a little haggling. Use the simple negotiating techniques described below and you should be able to get your RV at a great price.

Note that not a single one of the following statements say that you won't pay the price being asked. You imply it, but you don't actually say it. You are always free to accept the price that the seller is asking.

Here are my 7 all-time favorite negotiating phrases for people who don't like to negotiate

A lot of people don't like to negotiate, but when it comes to houses, cars, and RVs you have to. Sellers expect it and they don't quote you their best price to start with. In most cases, the seller (dealer or individual) doesn't realistically expect you to pay their asking price.

Negotiating doesn't have to be a hassle or an unpleasant experience. Just use one or more of the seven statements below and watch the asking price start to decrease in a hurry. If you use these statements, negotiating can be a fun experience.

#1. ALWAYS, ALWAYS flinch at the first price or proposal

You should almost fall over because you are so shocked. Do this even if the price you hear is way less than you expected. Flinch and say, "That's WAY out of my budget," and then shut up. Don't say a word. Just sit and wait for the price to drop.

#2. Next, when you get the lower price quote, you should say, "You've got to do better than that."

And again, you shut up. If you open your mouth, you won't get the next price concession. If you say yes to the first offer, the other person will know that they quoted you a price that was too low. They may even try to find a way to increase the price. They may say something like, "Well, let me see if the boss will go along with this price," or, "Let me make sure that this is ok with my wife."

#3. If you make a counter offer, ALWAYS ask for a much lower price than you expect to get.

One of the cardinal rules of negotiating is that you should ask the other side for more than you expect to get. Henry Kissinger went so far as to say, "Effectiveness at the negotiating table depends upon overstating one's demands."

#4. Never offer to split the difference

It's human nature to want to "play fair." Our sense of fair play dictates to us that if both sides give equally, then that's fair. Realize that the other side is almost always willing to split the difference, so you should try to get a slightly better deal than that.

#5. How to use two powerful negotiating techniques all in one sentence. The two techniques are: "Absent higher authority" and "If I could, would you?"

We've all experienced the "Absent higher authority" technique. For example, "Our insurance regulations won't let you go back in the shop," or "The loan committee wouldn't go along with those terms."

You don't get to talk to the loan committee (it doesn't exist) and you don't get to talk to the insurance company. It's a higher authority that you can't talk to.

Here's how to use the technique in your favor for once.

When you're down to the final negotiations, you can say, "If I could get my (financial adviser, spouse, or some absent higher authority) to go along with this, would you replace the two front tires?

Notice that, in this statement you haven't agreed to anything.

The owner or salesperson is in a position of feeling that they need to go along with what you're proposing to keep the deal from falling apart.

#6. Nibble for more at the end

You can usually get a little bit more even after you have basically agreed on everything—if you will use a technique called nibbling.

You can say, "You ARE going to have the carpets professionally cleaned (or you ARE going to replace the windshield wiper blades), aren't you?"

The sales person is already thinking about what he is going to do with his commission. The last thing he wants is for this sale to fall through. He will usually give just a little bit more if you "nibble."

#7. When you're getting close to the end of the negotiations and everything is just about nailed down, say, **"I'm getting nervous about this,"** and then **SHUT UP.** The other party will think the deal is about to fall apart and they will likely throw in one more concession to seal the deal.

One last point: If you're even remotely considering buying an RV, by all means, invest $2.99 and get a copy of Bill Myers' eBook, *How to Buy a Used Motorhome—How to get the most for your money and not get burned.* This book is about buying a used motorhome, but a lot of the information applies to buying a used camper/trailer. The book is also available as a printed book if you like printed books better than eBooks. They're both available on Amazon.

Bottom line: Do your research to determine what type of RV will be best for you. Then use the methods described in this chapter to find the RV you're looking for, and use some or all of the above negotiating techniques to get an even better price. Using these three techniques can cut the price you end up paying for your RV by thousands of dollars.

Chapter 8

Ways RVers Stretch Their Social Security

"It's nice to get out of the rat race, but you have to learn to get along with less cheese."

~ *Gene Perret*

Living the RV lifestyle is (or maybe I should say, it can be) much less expensive than living the conventional lifestyle. One important thing you have to remember is that moving into an RV won't automatically change who you are (or how you spend money). You have to make a conscious decision to change your habits.

Many RVers tell me that they spent a lot more money the first year they were on the road than they do now. A lot of new RVers try to do too much and travel too much. Slow down and relax. Everything will still be there next year.

The purpose of this chapter is to teach you how to immediately implement the techniques that it took many RVers a year or more to learn—that is, how to enjoy wine and roses on a water and daisy budget.

The 11 Common Ways RVers Stretch Their Dollars

1. **Going shopping is no longer a form of entertainment.** You only go shopping when you really need something and, even then, you consider buying what you need from Amazon. You can usually get a better price and you're not tempted to buy other stuff the way you would on a shopping trip.

2. **Buy clothes from Goodwill and thrift shops.** I bought two shirts from Goodwill recently for $4 each. One was an L.L. Bean shirt and one was a Lands End shirt. Both of these shirts retail for over $50. If you listen to the conversations around the campfire and at happy hour gatherings, you'll soon learn that a lot of full-time RVers shop for some of their clothes at Goodwill.

3. **You're not on a permanent vacation.** You can't take in all of the tourist attractions and stay on your budget. Searching out hiking trails and walking down the sidewalks in small towns is a popular form of entertainment for RVers.

4. **When you want to go out to eat, search out little mom and pop restaurants.** The big fancy restaurants where all of the tourists go are usually over priced, and I find that most of them are not unique. They are just cookie-cutter tourist restaurants. Fellow campers

sitting around the campfire will tell you where the hole-in-the-wall little restaurants are in the area that serve great local food at non-tourist prices. Tourist restaurants don't give you a flavor of the local area anyway. And, of course, don't go out to eat very often. Going out to eat should be a special event. Treat it that way and you will enjoy the experience a lot more.

5. **Don't waste food by putting leftovers in the refrigerator for a few days and then tossing them out.** Food is one of the biggest expenses in your budget so, naturally, it presents one of the biggest opportunities to save money. One of the best ways to save money is to not waste food by throwing it out. Plan most meals by looking at the leftovers that are in the refrigerator and then deciding what you will need to go with those leftovers to make a meal. If you don't want the same thing two meals in a row, at least plan to use the leftovers at the following meal. By all means, don't just put leftovers in the back of the refrigerator and forget about them for a few days. After all, RV refrigerators are small and it doesn't take many half-empty bowls to take up all of the room. Look at it this way: the more leftovers you eat, the more money there will be in the budget to go out to eat.

6. **Make it a habit to check eBay and craigslist before you buy almost anything.** Buying used (and sometimes new) items using eBay and craigslist can easily save you 50% or more on most items. I buy items on Amazon, too, but I usually find new items on Amazon and used items on eBay and craigslist. I bought new shocks for my motorhome on Amazon and I bought a used Progressive Industries portable electrical management system (a little box to protect against

electrical surges, open ground wires, low voltage, etc.) through eBay for about half of the retail price.

7. **Check out garage sales.** In addition to finding real bargains, going to garage sales is a great way to get to see the local area. I needed a 1¼ inch wrench to turn the ratchet that tightens the straps around the front tires when I put my car on the dolly to tow it. I had been using an adjustable wrench, but decided a wrench that would actually fit and one that had a longer handle would be a lot better. The problem was that a new wrench that big would be expensive. Sears had a wrench the size I needed for $27.49 plus tax. I found one at a yard sale for a dollar.

8. Another way to save money big-time is to **realize that things don't make you happy**. Think about all of the stuff that you will have to get rid of if you switch to the RV lifestyle. Think about all of the items you have bought that you don't use. When you're considering a purchase (whether it's an expensive item or a relatively inexpensive one), stop and think about whether you will really use it all that much and whether you will actually be happier a week or a month from now because you have it.

9. **Learning to be content with what you have** is one of the best ways in the world to save money—and it's a lot easier to do when you're living the RV lifestyle. RVers are not much into keeping up with the Joneses. Of course, there are big, fancy rigs, but for the most part, people consider that RVs are like pets. People don't even think about who has an expensive rig and who has a cheap rig any more than they think about who has an expensive dog and who has a rescue dog.

RVers' rigs (and dogs) are special and they love them both.

10. **Do some boondocking.** It's a great way to save money when traveling, and almost all RVers take advantage of it from time to time. RVs are completely self-contained and don't need to be connected to the world all the time. In fact, boondocking is such an important part of RVing that I have dedicated the next chapter to the subject.

11. **Do some of your own RV maintenance.** Instead of paying an RV service center $125 an hour or more, consider learning how to do some of the work yourself. You can get a mobile RV Technician to come out and spend a few hours with you and show you where a lot of things are and how to repair many routine items. Michael Witt is a master certified RV technician who owns **AshevilleRvRepair.com** and he offers a 4-hour one-on-one RV owner's maintenance course at your location. I took his course and learned a lot. I have already saved more in repair and service expenses than the course cost me. I'm sure mobile RV technicians in other areas offer the same service. If not, just hire one of them to come out for a few hours to go over everything with you. Having this knowledge will save you a lot of money in the long run. The more you know about your RV, the less money it will cost you to maintain it.

Don't get me wrong; I don't do all of the maintenance on my motorhome. For some things I take it to an RV service center that I trust. I have used Tom Johnson Camping Center in North Carolina (which is now owned by Camping World), and I have found them to be reliable, reasonable and very knowledgeable. I have even had them do work on my rig on Christmas Eve, and they stayed and got the work done.

One last point: There's a difference between being frugal and being cheap. Being frugal means that you show good judgment in the way you choose to spend your money. It's a mark of status today. It used to be that people kept it a secret when they bought something at Goodwill, now they brag about it.

Bottom line: By themselves, none of the techniques I've described in this chapter will work wonders with your budget, but when you use all of them on a consistent basis, the savings will really add up.

Chapter 9

Boondocking—the Art of Camping for Free

"A journey is like marriage. The certain way to be wrong is to think you control it."

~ John Steinbeck

Boondocking is the term used to describe camping or parking your RV where it's free. When you're boondocking you don't have access to electricity, water, or a sewer connection, but RVs are completely self-contained and don't need to be connected to the world all the time.

Since campground fees are a major part of your budget, spending some time boondocking is a great way for RVers to save a lot of money. Most RVers take advantage of it from time to time, and some RVers boondock almost all of the time.

Most RVs have a generator to charge the batteries and provide 120 VAC for the microwave, coffee pot, and air conditioners. Most of them also have an inverter that produces 120 VAC from the 12 volt batteries to charge computers, cell phones, run TVs, etc. Many RVers who do a lot of boondocking also add solar panels to the top of their RVs. Some have several solar panels and they don't even need a generator.

Solar panels are expensive, so I run my generator when I need to charge my batteries. I just push the button and crank up the generator. It needs to be run every now and then anyway. Of course, running the generator is not free; the generator uses about a dollar's worth of gas an hour when I'm running it to charge my batteries. (Of course, with a 5.5kw generator, I'm not putting anywhere near a full load on it. The manual says at full load it will use just a little less than a gallon an hour.)

I've found that I can keep my batteries charged by running my generator for about an hour a day. If I watched a lot of TV or used a lot of power, I'm sure I would need to run my generator more, but I've found that one hour a day seems to be adequate for me when I'm boondocking.

In addition to all of the electrical equipment, RVs have propane for heating, cooking, hot water, and running the refrigerator. They have a holding tank for fresh water, a holding tank for shower and sink water (which is called gray water), and a holding tank for the commode water (which is called black water).

The lighting is all 12 volts and works for days off of battery power. Having all LEDs makes the batteries last a lot longer before they have to be recharged. I changed all of my bulbs to LEDs about a year ago.

How many days you can go without connecting to the outside world mainly depends on how good you are at conserving water. If you're going to boondock much, you will need to learn how to take what's called a navy shower where you get wet, turn off the water and lather up and then turn it back on to rinse off. Also, you can't leave the water running all the time you're washing dishes. None of this is a problem if you're boondocking for two or three days and is only a concern if you plan to stay disconnected longer.

There are techniques you can use to extend the time you can stay disconnected from the world. Using a lot of these little techniques adds up. A useful tip is to have a bucket in the shower that you can use to run water in while you're waiting for the water to get hot. Then you have a bucket of water to use to wash dishes (you can heat it on your propane stove). If you just let the water run until it gets hot, you're using up your freshwater supply and you're also filling up your gray water holding tank.

I recently spent a week boondocking with two dozen other RVers in a cow pasture in south Florida. The purpose of the boondocking week was to have fun and learn from other, more experienced boondockers. There were some seminar type presentations and a lot of sitting around the campfire with other campers and discussing boondocking. I had a great time and I learned a lot.

One friend explained boondocking this way: He said, "I don't go to the grocery store unless I need groceries. I don't go to the barber shop unless I need a haircut. I don't go to the to service station unless I need gas. So why should I go to an RV park and pay $30 unless I need the services they provide?"

He said, "About once a week when I need to dump the holding tanks, charge my batteries, fill up my fresh water tank, and do laundry, I stop at an RV park for the night."

When I'm traveling and just want to stop for the night, my favorite boondocking place is a Walmart parking lot. They are everywhere, they're convenient and they're safe. I pull into a Walmart parking lot, fix supper, crank up the TV antenna and watch TV for a little while (using my batteries and inverter), and then go to bed. I don't have to bother with letting the jacks down, putting the slides out, or disconnecting the dolly so I can back into a camping space. The next morning I start the engine and hit the road. It's a very easy process. Boondocking on relocation days saves a lot of time, effort, and money. Of course, I have to remember to crank the TV antenna back down.

Most of the Flying J and Pilot truck stops are good options, too. (By the way, Flying J and Pilot have the same owners now.)

When it comes to traveling, a lot of campers use the 2-2-2 technique (or some variation of it). What this means is they don't drive more than 200 miles a day, they get to the next campground by 2:00 p.m., and they stay a minimum of two nights. This is a much more restful and enjoyable way to travel. Although I don't usually follow that technique, I do like to get to campgrounds by mid to late afternoon. I don't like to arrive after dark.

Here's a list of some popular places to boondock

- **Walmart parking lots:** As previously mentioned, this is the most popular place when traveling. About 90% of Walmart stores allow boondocking. Be sure to ask the manager for permission. Only stay one night—two at the most.

- **Cracker Barrel restaurants:** They have long, pull-through parking places behind the restaurants to accommodate trucks and RVs, and most of them will allow overnight parking, but be sure to get permission from the manager.

- **Movie theaters:** This is a little known boondocking place and is usually available except on the weekends. Again, ask for permission and while you're there, why not take in a movie. I'm sure the manager would appreciate it. In fact, the best way to get the manager to say, "Yes," is to say, "We're going to go to a movie and were wondering if it would be ok if we parked our RV in the back corner of your parking lot overnight?" This will get you approved almost every time. Of course, given the price of movies these days, you may not be saving much compared to staying in an RV park.

- **Truck stops:** Flying J is one of my favorites. Some truck stops have sewer dumps and most of them have a spigot where you can connect your hose and fill your freshwater tank. They have plenty of pull-through spaces. They are also safe. Be sure to fill up with gas while you're there and, of course, ask for permission to park overnight. I would ask for permission while I was parked at the gas pumps and before I filled up with gas. If they won't let you park overnight, go somewhere else to park and fill up with gas there.

- **Sam's Club**

- **Costco**

- **Lowe's**

- **Kmart**

- **Rest stops:** I like the ones that have full-time security. Even if they have a sign saying no overnight parking, ask the security guard or highway patrol officer and they will usually let you stay there.

- **Federal BLM (Bureau of Land Management) land:** You will find these mainly in the western part of the U.S. There are a few in the eastern part of the U.S., but not many.

- **FreeCampsites.net** is a website that has a list of free camping places. You can enter a city and state or a zip code and find campsites near you. In most cases, the website will include a lot of information about the sites. The best part about this website is that it's free to use.

- **Courtesy parking** is another option that RVers use. Courtesy parking is the term used to describe spending the night in a friend's driveway. It's kind of like 'couch surfing' except you don't use anyone's couch. If you stay more than one night, be sure to make yourself useful by mowing the grass, cooking dinner for the hosts, helping with a computer problem, taking their dog for a walk, etc. In other words, make yourself useful and you will be a welcome guest the next time you want to stop for a night or two.

Rules for boondocking in parking lots

Below are some rules (written and unwritten) that apply to boondocking in parking lots. Be sure to follow these rules. These rules don't apply in BLM areas.

- Ask the manager for permission.

- Don't put your leveling jacks down.

- Don't put the slides out (maybe just a little bit).

- Don't put the awnings out.

- Don't put lawn chairs out.

- Don't pull your grill out and start cooking.

- Don't run your generator.

In other words, you are "parking" and not really "camping." It's not actually required, but for common courtesy reasons try to buy things from the business while you're parked in their parking lot—things such as gas, groceries, supplies, etc. Since you're going to be buying these things anyway, why not buy from the businesses that are being nice to you.

Bottom line: Campground fees take a major bite out of your budget, so spending some time boondocking is a great way for RVers to save a lot of money. Mix some boondocking in with your stays at campgrounds and your monthly campsite expenses can be cut way down. That puts more money in the budget for gas.

Chapter 10

How to Supplement Your Social Security Income

"I told the doctor I broke my leg in two places. He told me to quit going to those places."

~ Henny Youngman

One of the biggest reasons many people are hesitant when it comes to making the decision to hit the road and live full time in their RV is the fact that they will no longer have a guaranteed income. Having a steady income provides a measure of security, and giving up that security can be scary.

This chapter is not about how to make a full-time living wage while living in your RV. I cover that topic on my website, LifeRV.com, and in my book, *Young RVers*. This chapter is about how to supplement your Social Security income.

What you have to do to make a lot of money is different from what you have to do to make a little extra money. And of course, making a lot of money usually takes a lot more of your time than making a little money to supplement your Social Security income.

By a little money, I'm talking about ways to make $200, $300, or maybe $500 a month. Yes, you can use the techniques described here and, by putting more effort into the endeavors, you can make more than $500 a month, but I'm guessing that you want to make a little bit of extra money while only putting in a little bit of effort. You don't want to work 30 or 40 hours a week.

Two ways RVers make supplemental income—Workamping jobs and as an Entrepreneur

I'm sure you have heard a lot about people who have an online business doing something they're passionate about and making lots of money. Maybe you can do that too, and I'll discuss some of these entrepreneurial techniques later in this chapter, but first, let's look at some guaranteed ways of making some supplemental income that don't involve the risk of running a business.

Workamping

The easiest, most common, and surest way to make money as a full-time RVer is to do what is called, "work-camping" (commonly referred to by the trademarked word, workamping™).

In a nutshell, this means working at a job where you get free camping in exchange for working 20 to 25 hours a week, and in many cases you will also receive a small salary (usually $8 to $12 an hour). If you can fog a mirror (and pass a drug test), you are almost guaranteed to be able to get one of these jobs any time you want it. You won't get rich, but you will be able to supplement your Social Security income, and that's what this chapter is all about.

Workamping jobs?

CoolWorks.com is one of the most popular websites RVers use to find jobs. You can check them out at the link below, and if you want to go directly to the jobs that provide RV spaces, the second link below will take you there without you having to do a bunch of clicking on their website.

CoolWorks.com

Coolworks.com/jobs-with-rv-spaces

Here are two more popular websites that RVers use to find jobs:

Work-For-RVers-and-Campers.com

Workamper.com

There is a subscription charge to see the information at the Workamper.com website, but the other websites I've listed are free.

If you want to work in one of the national parks, your best bet would be to work for one of the concessionaires who contract to provide services to the national parks. Delaware North, Xanterra, Forever Resorts, and Aramark are four popular concessionaire contractors.

You could also work for the Yellowstone Association, the Grand Canyon Association, or other national park association. You can find job openings on one or more of the websites listed above.

You could work for the National Park Association directly, but for most of those jobs, they want a one-year commitment.

The most popular workamping job
One of the most popular workamping jobs for RVers is working in one of Amazon's four fulfillment centers from early fall through Dec. 23rd. Amazon has a big need for people to pack boxes during the pre-Christmas season. With this job you will stand a lot and walk a lot, but you get free camping and the pay is good—$10 to $12 an hour. You also get overtime pay, plus a $1 an hour bonus if you stay until Dec. 23rd. Check out the opportunity at the link below:

AmazonFulfillmentCareers.com/opportunities/camper-force

To get the best jobs, I recommend that you go online and fill out an application six months or so in advance. It's a good idea to apply for more than one job and at more than one location. That way you will likely have several jobs to choose from.

After you send in your application, you will be interviewed by phone within a week or two—sometimes within a day or two. About the only requirements are that you need to pass a drug test and you must have a high school diploma or equivalent in most cases.

Keep in mind that with some workamping jobs you only work 20 to 25 hours a week and just get free camping. In others you work 30 to 40 hours a week and you get free (or reduced-rate) camping, plus a salary for the hours you work. Be sure you know which type of job you're applying for.

Other options: With many (if not most) campgrounds it's possible to work out an arrangement to camp for free in exchange for working 20 to 25 hours a week. They may not have a formal program, but talk to the owner/manager and in many cases you can work something out. I know several RVers who do this all the time. It's usually easier to get these positions by applying in person while you're staying at the campground. KOA campgrounds have a worker program, and they even let you stay free at other KOA campgrounds while you're traveling between jobs.

Also, most state parks have a limited number of openings for free camping when you volunteer and work 20 to 25 hours a week. Usually there is no salary with these jobs, but you get to camp free in some beautiful places—beaches, mountains, etc. Be sure to apply for these jobs six months or so in advance to get to camp in the most popular areas.

What would you be doing if you had a Workamping job?
Basically, if you workamp in national parks, state parks, or private campgrounds, the work will usually consist of chores like cleaning bathrooms, riding around on an ATV showing campers where their camping spaces are, working in a gift shop, etc. This is not hard work at all. When you're working for Amazon, doing sugar beet harvesting (or working anywhere where the company is trying to make a profit), you will be expected to work a lot harder (and usually get paid more). Keep this in mind when you're deciding what type of work you want to do.

One good thing about these jobs is that they are all low stress. There's no office politics. You just do your work and go home. The jobs usually last two to four months at a time and you are free to leave anytime you want to.

Here are some of the jobs RVers I know have had recently:

- Retail clerk

- Office work

- Interpreter

- Campground host

- Tram driver

- Pointing out eagles and other wildlife at a National Park

- Guest services and maintenance at a resort ranch

- Working as a guide at a lighthouse

- Working in a gift shop—cashier, stocking, etc.

- Packing boxes for Amazon during the three months before Christmas.

- Gatekeepers at oil fields. Two RVers park their RVs at the gate and rotate 12-hour shifts letting trucks in and out. The hours are long, but the pay is above average for workamping jobs.

- Sugar beet harvesting. This is very hard work, but way above average pay. Check it out at SugarBeetHarvest.com

What a lot of RVers do is work at Amazon for a few months in the fall and then that's enough supplemental income to allow them not to have to work the other months of the year. Some RVers buckle down and do this hard work for a few months and then do some camp hosting or other light work off and on during the rest of the year in exchange for free camping.

Do you want to be an Entrepreneur?

Workamping jobs are a common way for RVers to make a little extra money and/or get free camping. If you want to make more than just a little extra money, below are some entrepreneurial techniques that usually take more of your time and don't necessarily guarantee that you will be successful, but they do have the possibility of providing a much larger income than workamping.

A lot of RVers use a little of both techniques. They do some workamping jobs so they will have a small guaranteed income and a free place to camp while they're working to get one or more of these other incoming-producing techniques up and running.

Popular entrepreneurial income-producing endeavors RVers use

There has never been an easier way to make money working at home (even if your home is an RV) than by working with your computer. Some people just use their computer to sell their services or to sell the items they're making at home—jewelry, paintings, baskets, etc.

Technically-minded people use their computers to do what is called computer work—designing websites, doing graphic design work, Photoshop editing, computer programing, creating apps, etc. Others are using their computers to run online businesses selling items on eBay or Amazon, or to write books, or produce videos to monetize on YouTube.

Don't fall for any of the work-at-home schemes you see advertised or the ones you get spam email messages about. Use the information in this chapter and do your own thing.

I talked to a lady the other day when I was parked next to to her when I was boondocking for the night in a Walmart parking lot. She had just paid $13,000 for a franchise to sell LEDs. That didn't include any inventory of LEDs. The plan was that she would go out and find businesses that needed their lights replaced with LEDs. I wish her well, but at the time I was talking to her she had not sold any LEDs yet.

I sell LEDs, but I didn't pay anyone a franchise fee to get started. I buy 2,000 LEDs at a time from China and sell them on Amazon. I package them in Ziplock™ bags and send them all to Amazon and use their FBA program and let them do all of the order taking and shipping.

My advice is to be very careful when it comes to investing in a business opportunity or a work-at-home scheme.

Ways RVers are using their computers to make money
The many ways people are using their computers to make money amazes me. It seems as though I meet people almost every week who are using their computers to make money in ways I had never thought of.

Create a website and sell your own products: This week I talked to a mother and daughter team who were working at home, hand-winding electronic pickup devices for musical instruments. They were selling the items on their own website, on eBay, and on Amazon. They were making enough to support both of them, plus pay the daughter's way through college.

Buy and sell items on craigslist: One thing that a lot of people do to make money is to buy and sell items on craigslist. Stick to items you know something about and are interested in. Some of the things people are buying and selling are musical instruments, bicycles, antiques, toys, etc.

Do freelance creative design work: There are four major websites that help you get jobs (or gigs as they are called).

- Elance.com

- Odesk.com (renamed Upwork.com)

- Freelancer.com

- Fiverr.com

You can offer to do all kinds of work on each site, but each one more or less specializes in a certain field, like computer programming, graphic design, etc. To read a review of the differences between Odesk, Elance and Freelancer, take a look at the review at the link below:

blog.hubstaff.com/odesk-vs-elance-vs-freelancer

By the way, Odesk and Elance have recently merged, but they still run two separate websites, so for all practical purposes, they are still two different businesses.

Make money posting videos on YouTube

Here's one more way to make money with your computer. Post videos on YouTube and select the "Monetization" option. The way this works is that YouTube will place ads on the website with your video and then pay you when people click on the ads.

If you don't see the Monetization option when you upload your video, it means that you have not linked your Google AdSense account to your YouTube account. That's easy to do as long as you have used the same email address for both accounts.

YouTube will pay you about $1,000 for every 100,000 clicks. That comes out to about one cent per click. It depends on the topic. I haven't done much with YouTube, but I do have one video that has had over 115,000 views. I need to get busy and put up a bunch more videos. That's the next project on my to-do list.

Important point about making money with YouTube videos: YouTube likes winners. As I said before, you might expect to earn $1,000 if your video received 100,000 views in one month, but if you had 10 videos and each one received 10,000 views, your income might be only $50 or $100. To make money, you have to post videos that get a lot of views and, by a lot, I mean 100,000 or more a month.

Some people make more than a million dollars a month from their YouTube videos. Some of the most profitable videos are simple 3-minute videos demonstrating Disney toys.

If you want to get an idea of what topics get a lot of YouTube views, you can see the top 100 moneymakers on YouTube at the link below:

SocialBlade.com/youtube/top/country/US

Social Blade is a website dedicated to tracking YouTube statistics. You can use the site to track your own success with YouTube.

Unless you really hit it big, you probably won't make a lot of money from any one video, but if you continue to upload videos, you might be surprised at how much you could make every month. I have a friend who received more than $4,000 in one month recently from a single video.

It doesn't take fancy, high-priced video equipment to make these videos. You will need a video camera that has an external microphone jack and you'll need a $29 external lavalier mic. Don't use the built-in microphone on the video camera, the sound will be terrible. You would also most likely need a tripod to hold the camera. You will probably need one or two lights. Use the daylight type fluorescent bulbs. That's it. In most cases, you will need a video-editing program (like Sony Movie Studio) to do some editing on your videos. You can get version 12 of Sony Movie Studio for $29 now and, in my opinion, that's better than the later, more expensive versions.

Write books and sell them using Amazon. When you write a book, make it available in both the Kindle eBook format and in printed format. Novels sell a lot better than how-to books, but writing novels is not my area of expertise, so I stick to writing how-to books. I have written 10 books. Some of my books don't bring in much income at all and some of them bring in $1,000 or more a month. I have a friend who has books that bring in $3,000 or more a month—but those are novels.

The good thing about books is that they continue to bring in money month after month with no additional work on your part. Even "not much money per book" multiplied by several books adds up to a good supplemental income and, who knows, you might end up with a book that brings in a lot of money each month.

I use Fiverr.com to find a graphic designer to design my book covers and I also used Fiverr.com to find Ken, the proofreader and editor that I use to proof and edit my books. You can find him at the link below:

Fiverr.com/mrproofreader

If you want to learn even more about how to make money while living in an RV, check out my website at LifeRV.com for my latest articles on the topic.

Bottom line: In this chapter I've described several proven jobs (including how to get those jobs) and some other income-producing techniques that other full-time RVers are using to supplement their income. You don't have to choose just one moneymaking endeavor. You can have multiple streams of income—that's what I do.

Chapter 11

Logistics—Domicile, Mail, Banking, Pets, etc.

"You've got a lot of choices. If getting out of bed in the morning is a chore and you're not smiling on a regular basis, try another choice."

~ *Steven D. Woodhull*

Even if you're full time on the road, you still have to have a legal physical address. Where do you get your mail? Where do you vote? Where do you pay taxes on your RV and vehicle? What address is on your driver's license? The list goes on and on.

Which state should you select for your legal domicile?

The easy answer is that if you're going to keep your house or have property where you live now and plan to spend a lot of time there, you can just keep your address in the city and state you're living in now. Get a local mail forwarding service or get a friend or relative to let you use their address as your legal address.

That is the easiest way, but it may not be the best way to do it. If you're going to be receiving earned income, you may want to select a state that doesn't have state income tax. And there are other reasons to consider selecting a state other than where you now live.

Lawyers like to be picky with words, and the word that's important to them is that you are choosing a state as your **domicile**. What's special about your domicile is that it's where you **intend** to make your permanent home. It doesn't matter where you're residing right now, but where do you intend to make your home when you come to your senses and decide to settle down—just kidding about coming to your senses, but you get the point.

A note about state income tax: If you have income through the Internet, selling books, etc., you will report that income in your domicile state and if that state doesn't have any state income tax, then you won't pay any state tax on that income.

But if you're working for Amazon or some company that hands you a paycheck, you will get a W-2 or 1099 form at the end of the year and you will have to file (and pay) taxes in that state for that portion of your income. If you have worked in several states during the year, you will end up having to file state tax returns in several states.

If you're doing workamping in exchange for a free camping site, this is not considered income and you don't pay taxes on the value of the campsite. Even if you're working for a state or national campground, you don't get a W-2 or 1099 for the value of your campsite. I'm not an accountant or tax lawyer and this is not tax advice—it's just my understanding of how the system works.

States with no state income tax:

- Alaska

- Florida

- Nevada

- South Dakota

- Texas

- Washington

- Wyoming

- Tennessee and New Hampshire don't tax earned income, but they do tax interest and dividend income.

There are other things to consider. If you're buying a high-priced RV, you can save thousands of dollars if you register it in a state that has low or no sales tax or personal property tax.

The three states most RVers consider
There's no one perfect state, but here are the three RV-friendly states that are the most popular with RVers.

Florida because:

- There is no state tax on earned income or investments.

- It's convenient for RVers who plan to spend a lot of time on the East Coast.

- Vehicle insurance is reasonable—not the lowest, but for sure not the highest.

Texas because:

- There is no state income tax.

- Driver's licenses can be renewed by mail.

- You can register to vote by mail.

- Vehicle registration fees are low, but you do have to get your vehicles inspected every year. (If you're out of state when your inspection expires, you have 30 days after you get back in the state to get your rig inspected.)

South Dakota because:

- There is no state income tax.

- There is no state vehicle inspection, so you don't have to go back each year, but you do have to go back every five years and renew your driver's license in person. (You can renew your driver's license once by mail.)

- Vehicle insurance is much lower than in most states—as much as 50% less than some states.

- There is only a 3% excise tax and no sales tax to pay. This could save you a lot if you're buying a high-priced RV.

- To get a driver's license or renew one in South Dakota, RVers are required to spend a minimum of one night in a campground in South Dakota and bring a receipt from the campground proving that they spent the night there.

- South Dakota is no longer considered to be a good choice for RVers who are not on Medicare. The new healthcare laws make it almost impossible to get affordable coverage in South Dakota if you don't live there at least six months out of the year.

One word of caution: Don't choose any state that you only plan to visit once every five years or so to get your driver's license renewed. If you're from an aggressive tax state like New York (and many other states are getting aggressive about taxes now) and you have only been to the state you selected for your domicile once for three days in the last five years, it might be hard to convince a court that your intentions are to make that state your home—and what your intentions are is what's important when it comes to proving which state is your domicile.

In addition to getting things set up in your new state, you need to make sure the state that is currently your legal residence knows that you are leaving.

The more things you can do to make a clean break with your previous state the better. Also, when selecting which state will be your domicile, keep in mind that you may be called for jury duty from time to time.

Things you can do to make it clear that you are no longer a resident of your previous state

If you sell your home and all real estate, that makes a big statement, but that's not absolutely necessary.

If you decide to rent a storage building, rent it in your new state if possible.

Get a legal address through a mail forwarding service in your new domicile state and change your address for all of the things listed below.

A partial list of things to switch to your new legal address

Driver's License

Voter Registration

Insurance (Life, Health, RV and Auto)

Social Security Administration

Medicare

IRS

Credit Cards

Bank Accounts and Brokerage Accounts

Car and RV Registration

Change your address online everywhere it's recorded—Facebook, your eBay account, Amazon, any discussion forums you're on, any profiles, etc.

Since you have to declare and set up a legal address, the sooner you do it the better. So, as the comedian Larry the Cable Guy, says, "Git-R-Done."

The reason you have to go through all of these steps is that your present state would like for you to continue paying taxes in their state. When there's a lot of money involved, states have brought lawsuits (and won sometimes) claiming that someone was a resident of their state.

Don't try to have it both ways

Don't take financial advantages of having an address in your previous state—such as discounts at state parks when camping there.

If your situation is anything other than straight-forward or if there's a lot of money involved (such as a large amount of income or potentially large inheritance taxes, etc.), I recommend that you consult with an experienced domicile attorney.

Getting your mail

Every state has companies that provide mail forwarding services. The companies listed below are RV friendly and they offer services to scan your mail and send you a picture of the outside of the envelope. They will forward the mail to you that you want forwarded and shred the junk mail that you don't want forwarded. These services will also open your mail and scan the inside for you if you sign up for this service—for an extra fee, of course.

Here's a partial list of mail forwarding companies in the three most popular states that RVers select as their domicile state

This list is not complete. There are others, but the companies listed below cater to RVers and have a lot of positive reviews from RVers. Of course, you have to select a service that's in the state you selected as your domicile state.

Florida:

- MyRvMail.com – You get a discount with this service if you're a member of Passport America (which gives you a 50% discount on 1,900 campgrounds). They are located in Crestview, FL.

- AmHomeBase.com – American Home Base, Inc. is located in Pensacola, FL, and is associated with Good Sam's.

- SbiMailService.com – St. Brendan's Isle, located just outside of Jacksonville, FL, in Green Cove Springs, FL. I've talked to a lot of RVers who use their services and they all give this company great recommendations.

Texas:

- EscapeesRV.com – Escapees RV Club is located in Livingston, TX. They offer their members a lot of services in addition to a mail forwarding service. They have a network of 1,000 RV parks that offer discounts on camping for their members. Also, they are associated with companies that provide discounts for RV insurance, medical insurance, banking, and loans. You don't have to have Texas as your domicile to be a member. You can be a member and use another company in your domicile state for your mail forwarding service.

South Dakota:

- Americas-Mailbox.com – They're located in Rapid City, SD. They have a good reputation and many RVers like their friendly and personal service.

Before visiting any state to get your domicile set up, be sure to contact the company you're going to be using as your mail forwarding service and find out what you will need to bring. You will probably need to bring your birth certificate and maybe some other papers. Find out before you go.

Voting

You need to get registered to vote. You will vote in the precinct where your legal address is. In some states you can register to vote when you get your driver's license. And when elections come up, you need to vote in both local elections and in national elections. This helps establish that you are participating in activities in your new state. You can vote using an absentee ballot.

Be sure to take your name off the voter registration list for the state you're moving from. That will be one more thing that will help establish the fact that your previous state is no longer your domicile state.

Banking

As a full-time RVer, my opinion is that you need accounts with at least two different, unrelated banks. When passwords or debit cards get lost or when there are problems of any kind with one account, having a second account could save you a lot of grief while you're getting things straightened out.

Also, when you're looking for a branch bank, if you have two banks, you are a lot more likely to find one close to you.

When selecting the two banking institutions, make sure they have branches in the states you plan to travel to the most. Online banks are a good option too now. I use Wells Fargo and Bank of America, but banks are all rapidly changing the services they offer, so do your homework before selecting your two banks.

Some features that you should look for when selecting banks include the ability to transfer money between accounts online, the ability to make payments online, and the ability to deposit checks by just making a picture of the check and sending it to them. In other words, you want a bank that is very much into online banking.

As a plan "C", you should keep some cash hidden in your RV. There are lots of places in an RV where you could have a few hundred dollars well hidden.

What about Pets and RVs?

In most campgrounds I would say that about half of the RVs have a dog (or should I say that the dog has an RV?). I don't know if any of the dogs actually drive their RV, but most of them seem to be in charge and run the show.

Seriously, pets make great companions when traveling and living the RV lifestyle. They enjoy checking out new places and seeing new things. Even cats that stay inside all of the time seem to enjoy and be intrigued by the new scenery.

Almost all campgrounds allow pets. There are some rules that must be followed, so make sure you and your pet both read the rules. The rules are usually straight-forward, common sense rules such as, no barking, your dog must be on a leash, clean up after your pet, etc.

What do you do about a vet?

First of all, be sure to keep current copies of all of your pet's vaccinations or you might end up getting duplicate and unnecessary treatments. One solution is to use a national chain of vets such as Banfield Pet Hospital. They have offices all over the country. Go to their website at BanfieldPetHospital.com and enter the zip code where you are and you can find their closest office. Many of their offices are located inside PetSmart™ stores. They have a centralized database and your pet's records can be brought up at any of their offices.

When traveling with pets, you just have to pay a little bit of attention to their special needs—especially when you're away from the RV for a few hours. Make sure it doesn't get too hot or too cold, and make sure they have plenty of water.

One last point about traveling with pets

Be sure to keep plenty of your pet's food on hand. You may not be able to find your normal brand everywhere (even if it's a common brand). Changing your pet's food and then hitting the road in your RV could result in trouble for you and your pet. Don't risk it. Some people order their favorite brand of pet food on Amazon and have it shipped to wherever they are, if it's a brand that's not commonly available.

The logistics of getting ready for RVing are not as hard as they seem

The job of handling all of the details discussed in this chapter is not hard. It's just 101 little things that you have to do. Make sure you jump through all of the hoops to clearly establish your new state as your domicile. Most of the time, it's never a problem—especially, if there's not a lot of tax money involved, so don't let all of my cautions scare you.

The worst thing that could happen is that you have to pay the taxes you would have had to pay if you had not done anything. In other words, it's heads you win and tails you don't lose.

On second thought, it could be worse. As one attorney explained it to me, if your previous home state could prove that you never really intended for the new state to be your domicile, you would owe not only back taxes, but also penalties and interest from when you first started saying you were a resident of the new state. This could really add up.

Bottom line: Take the time to decide which state will be your legal domicile, get your mail forwarding service set up, your banking, voter registration, car and RV titles and registration taken care of, and, of course, get your driver's license changed over, and then get your address changed everywhere it's recorded. In other words, do everything outlined and recommended in this chapter.

Nothing about all of this is hard, it's just a lot of little things that need to be done, but these things are easy to put off. Get them done.

Chapter 12

How to Get Healthcare on the Road

"My doctor gave me six months to live, but when I couldn't pay the bill, he gave me six months more."

~ Walter Matthau

Getting health care when you don't really live anywhere in particular can be a little challenging.

The biggest problem is finding a plan that won't get you caught up in having to find doctors in your network. If you're old enough to be on Medicare (with or without a supplement plan), things are a lot easier.

107

If you're not old enough for Medicare

If you're not old enough to be on Medicare, things get a lot more complicated when it comes to getting affordable medical care as an RVer.

If you go with the Affordable Care Act (also called ACA or ObamaCare), there are some hoops you will have to jump through because the problem of finding doctors can be difficult as, in many cases, you will have a small network of doctors.

Here are some of the things you need to consider:

- Some companies don't insure RVers. It's written in their policy, so this is a deal killer. Check this first and if you find this restriction, stop and look for another company.

- Next check the details of the plan's network. Will it cover you in all 50 states or just a few? If it's just a few, are these the states that you plan to be in most of the time?

- What about the out-of-network benefits? Some plans don't cover much when you're out of network except for emergency services. And most plans have a much higher deductible when you're out of network.

- Some plans require you to prove you are a resident of the state by showing a utility bill or other proof—avoid these plans.

- Some plans require you to live in a state for at least six months of each year—avoid these plans.

- Avoid HMO plans and stick with PPO plans that have a large nationwide network of providers. This is a good idea as a general rule because HMOs restrict you to a small network of providers, but they are a lot less expensive. Going with an HMO instead of a PPO is in general not a good idea, but it depends on your travel plans and the risks you're willing to take. In one case, a fellow RVer told me that a PPO plan was three times as expensive, so he went with an HMO since it would cover emergencies out of network and if he had a serious medical problem, he would travel back to a doctor or hospital in his network. In other words, there are a lot of factors to consider. Do your homework.

• You will need to decide if you want to go with the in exchange (also called Obamacare or ACA) or buy your own insurance out of exchange. Also, if you go with an ACA in exchange plan, you will need to find out if you qualify for a subsidy. Here is a link to a website that has a handy tool to provide estimates of health insurance premiums and subsidies for people purchasing insurance on their own in health insurance exchanges created by the ACA (Affordable Care Act). kff.org/interactive/subsidy-calculator

• The state you select as your domicile will determine which plans are available to you. You may decide that another state (even with higher taxes) would be an overall better choice based on insurance choices and prices. You also may decide that the subsidies you would receive when going with an ACA plan may not be worthwhile because of the limited area of coverage and, if that's the case, you may decide that you would be better off with your own individual plan.

• Going with your own individual plan is a good option for some people. The annual deductible amounts that you have to pay out of your pocket are usually high ($1,000 to $5,000 or more), but they do cover the major expenses—surgeries, etc. So if you're reasonably healthy, this may be a good option for you. In other words, you will pay for your visits to a doctor for a sore throat, and the insurance will pay for medical expenses after you meet your deductible. Some of the companies that RVers have gone with include Blue Cross Blue Shield, Humana, Aetna, and Assurant. There are others, this is not a complete list.

- Look into policies that are eligible for a health savings account (HSA). This allows you to put up to $3,350 (in 2016) into a savings account and then use that money to pay for your out-of-pocket health expenses. In essence, you are paying your part of your health expenses with pre-tax dollars.

Short-term insurance is another option to consider

If you're reasonably healthy, you might want to consider what is called short-term insurance. It's the only plan that is allowed to be sold outside of ObamaCare (ACA) exchanges.

The premiums run at just over $100/month compared to about $270/month for traditional plans. In addition to its low cost, **one of the biggest benefits of short-term insurance for RVers is that you can go to see doctors anywhere.**

The plan doesn't cover pre-existing conditions, and the policy is for one year and renewal is not guaranteed.

If you stay healthy, you can renew the policy each year, but if you get sick and have expensive medical costs, the plan will cover your medical expenses until the end of the one-year period, and then you cannot renew your policy.

That's not all bad because you can then buy ACA insurance and insurers can't charge sick people any more than well people.

There is one minor problem with short-term insurance and that is that you will have to pay the tax penalty for not having ACA insurance. That's fine. It was only $95 for the whole year in 2015, but it went up to $695 a year or 2.5% of your income (whichever is greater) in 2016. That's still less than $58 a month.

Generally, if you're making less than $37,000 a year or have a serious pre-existing health problem, you would probably be better off going with ACA insurance, but, otherwise, consider short-term insurance as long as you're reasonably healthy, and then switch to ACA insurance later if you develop an expensive health problem.

How to buy ACA insurance if you missed signing up during an open enrollment period

If you missed the Open Enrollment period, you may still be able to buy Marketplace coverage by taking advantage of what is called a Special Enrollment Period. If you get married, have a baby or move, you will have 60 days to report what is called a "life-changing event." And then you'll get a new eligibility notice.

The keyword in the above explanation for RVers is the word "move." If you change your domicile state, that is considered a move to a different state.

Sources for more health insurance information

Kyle Henson is a licensed insurance agent and a fellow full-time RVer. I'm not associated with him in any way, but his website has a wealth of insurance information for RVers, and I've heard a lot of RVers say good things about the services he provides. I recommend that you take a look at the information on his website to help you make your decision concerning what to do about finding affordable health insurance. Here is his website:

RVerInsurance.com

In addition to the above information, the following website allows you do comparison shopping of exchange policy plans: TheHealthSherpa.com.

Even though you have insurance, getting an appointment with a doctor in a city where you have never been to a doctor before could be a problem. Some doctors don't take new patients and some have a waiting list.

Three techniques RVers use to get to see a doctor

1. Some RVers make use of Emergency Medical Clinics (also called a "Doc-in-a-box") or use a service like Teladoc.com when they have a minor medical problem—sore throat, etc.

2. With Teladoc, you can place a call and a board-certified doctor will call you back (usually within about 15 minutes). The doctor can discuss your symptoms with you, and then call in a prescription to a pharmacy near you, if necessary, or tell you if they think you need to see a specialist. You can pay the fee out of

your health savings account funds. Some insurance policies cover this expense.

3. A third option is that CVS, Walgreens, and some other pharmacies now have a nurse practitioner on staff part of the time. You can walk in, and immediately they can examine you and then write a prescription for you for minor health problems, if necessary, or tell you that you need to see a specialist.

Bottom line: Your goal should be to look at your health condition, your travel plans, your budget, and then select the health insurance plan that meets your RVing lifestyle needs. It's not as complicated as it first seems. Just look at the facts, use the resources and guidelines outlined in this chapter, and make your decision.

Note that the government is changing health insurance rules all the time, so be sure to check the latest rules.

Chapter 13

The Emotional Aspects of Full-time RVing

"Obstacles are those frightful things you see when you take your eyes off your goal."

~ Henry Ford

You can look at the numbers until you're blue in the face. On paper everything looks like it will work out great, but you still have that uneasy feeling in your gut. Questions such as, "Will I be happy? Will it work? What if?" keep popping into your head.

Taking the plunge into the full-time RV lifestyle is a major life-changing event. All RVers have these feelings, and they experience a flood of emotions when they're contemplating taking the leap. The feelings are normal, but you have to deal with them, and the best way to deal with them is to be prepared for them and be expecting them.

When you announce your plans to your family and friends, they will throw up even more questions, doubts, and fears for you to consider.

There will be doubts and questions all along the way—when you announce your plans, while you're preparing to make the transition, and even after you get on the road.

Questions that may haunt you from time to time

As you think about living full-time in an RV and make plans to hit the road, you can expect a barrage of last-minute questions to pop into your head. This is normal, but if you've done your homework and gone through the numbers and know that it will work, don't let these questions discourage you.

Here are some of the questions you can expect:

- Am I being realistic?

- Will this really work?

- Will my family and friends think I'm crazy?

- Will I be lonely?

- Is this a mistake?

When you hear these questions in your head, think of what some wise people have had to say about life, as stated in their quotes below:

Whenever you find yourself on the side of the majority, it's time to pause and reflect.

~ *Mark Twain*

Your life does not get better by chance, it gets better by change.

~ *Jim Rohn*

"When in doubt, choose change."

~ *Lily Leung*

Reflecting on some of these famous quotes will help convince you that you're making the right choice. After all, you've already gone through the numbers, and you know from a logical standpoint that you're making the right decision.

The emotional part of getting on the road comes down to five areas

1. Selling your home or moving out of your apartment
Downsizing from a traditional house or apartment can seem scary and overwhelming. Women seem to have a harder time with this than men. What if you change your mind? Maybe you could keep your house and rent it out. If you need the equity in your house to buy your RV, it's a simple

decision—you either sell it or you stay put. It's not an easy decision, but it is a simple one.

If you're leaving an apartment that you're renting, it's a lot less stressful. This is a personal matter, but go through the numbers, make the decision and then live with the emotions. Most people tell me it's a very liberating feeling when the house is sold and they are free to enjoy the RV lifestyle.

One other thing to think about is, you're probably ready for a change or you wouldn't even be considering the RV lifestyle. And even if you later decide you don't like the RV lifestyle, you probably won't want to go back to your previous life or to the exact same house or apartment that you're unhappy with now.

2. Getting rid of your stuff

The logistics of how to get rid of your stuff were covered earlier. I talked about the techniques that would make the process easy, but I didn't talk about the emotions involved with the process. This is the one area that gives people a lot of worry and has them asking, "What if?"

The truth of the matter is I have never talked to anyone who said they miss all of that stuff. In fact, I don't remember anyone ever saying that they miss a single item. It's such a load off of them when all of that stuff is gone. You could put all of your stuff in storage, but that gets expensive. If you feel that you have to put everything in storage, it probably means you're not ready to simplify your life.

If you're having trouble getting rid of your stuff, go back and re-read chapter 5 and follow the simple steps outlined. That's how I got rid of my stuff, and the technique worked amazingly quick and easy.

3. How to deal with your family's reactions when you announce your plans

Some will think you've lost your mind, some will be envious, and some will think it's a phase that you will soon grow out of and be back home to settle down.

When you announce your plans to your family and friends, be prepared to answer some questions. Here is the one big question you need to be prepared to answer (after all, you need to be able to answer this question for yourself, too):

How will you support yourself without depleting your savings? Explain that, because the cost of living the RV lifestyle is less than the cost of how you're living now, your Social Security check (or checks, if there are two of you) will cover your basic expenses. Then explain the concept of workamping and how having that option will allow you to travel more or have extra income anytime you choose to go that route. Also, explain how technology now allows you to earn supplemental income and have location-independent streams of income. Maybe go into some of the Internet projects you're considering (if you're thinking about going that route), things like selling on Amazon or eBay, or some of the other options discussed in chapter 10 about how to supplement your Social Security income.

4. Dealing with being away from family and friends

This turns out to be not nearly as difficult as most people expect it to be. With email, Skype, and cell phones you can stay in touch as much as you want to—there just won't be as much face-time. You will stay in touch with a few of your previous friends, but not as many as you think—mainly because you won't have as much in common with them as you do now.

You will find that you will be spending a lot more time with your new RV friends because you will have so much more in common with them. I've heard several RVers say that they have a lot more friends now that they're living the RV lifestyle than they ever had when they lived in a traditional house or apartment.

5. Feelings to expect after you get on the road

You'll be questioning yourself for a while after you hit the road. This is normal. The future is unknown, but realistically, it's unknown in your present lifestyle, too.

Accept the fact that the emotions and doubts you feel when you first start out are normal. They will fade quickly when the excitement kicks in. How can you feel down when every day is a new adventure?

From time to time if you need to go through all of the reasons you wanted to live the RV lifestyle and go over all of the numbers again that you crunched to make sure it would work, it's fine to do it, but at some point you have to accept the fact that, here you are. Enjoy the journey.

You always have the option to go back to your previous life, but give it a year. My bet is that going back will not happen—at least, not anytime soon.

The next phase—the emotional part of being on the road

In addition to the emotions you will experience while you're getting ready to hit the road, there will be emotions to deal with once you're on the road too.

Knowing what to expect and being prepared for the emotional parts of RV life will help you be able to handle (and enjoy) this lifestyle.

Being away from and missing family and friends can be difficult to adjust to, but it can be made much easier by making use of the following opportunities:

- Make use of Skype for face-to-face time. It's almost like being with the other person, and in some ways even better because you have their undivided attention.

- Arrange to have family visit you in a fun location for a few days or a week.

- Arrange your travel plans so you can visit family and friends for a few days or a week or so from time to time. With your RV parked in their driveway or at a nearby RV park, you both have your own space.

- Make it a point to be at special occasions.

Face the fact that there will be a huge emotional challenge when you leave your home. Leaving your home, job, family, and friends all at once can be a big blow. Yes, it can be down-right scary. Accept this feeling as normal.

Instead of making one big leap, some people think about putting their stuff in storage and renting out their house for a year so they can come back to it if they change their minds. My thoughts are that if you think you're ready for a change, you probably are. You may find that the RV lifestyle is not the change you want, but I'm betting that going back to the life you left is not it either.

If you decide the RV life is not the life for you, you will be ready to move on to something else—a different town, a different house or apartment, living on a boat, or maybe even living in a different country. I lived in Costa Rica for six months and thoroughly enjoyed it. Whatever you decide to do, I'm betting that living the conventional lifestyle you're living now is not how you want to live the rest of your life.

Meeting new friends

As many fellow RVers predicted, and as I have found out, I have a lot more friends now that I'm living full time in my motorhome than I had before. You'll find that, since all RVers are away from their family and friends, they are all looking to meet new friends. RVers are a friendly bunch.

You will be welcome at happy hour and around the campfire, and it doesn't matter what size rig you have. Even if you only see these new friends for a few days and don't stay in touch with them much afterwards, you may see them months (or a year) later. When you do see these people again, you will be greeted like a long-lost friend. It's just the RV way.

You will meet new friends and then see them several times a year—even dog-legging out of your way to meet up with them from time to time.

One last point, when two people are in an RV 24/7 with only each other to talk with, you better believe they will welcome someone new to talk to. Maybe that's the reason RVers are so friendly.

Bottom line: Yes, you will have to deal with a lot of emotions when it comes to embarking on the RV lifestyle. Consider your emotions and let them guide you to go over and over your plans and decisions, but if the numbers say you can do it and it's what you want to do, don't let fear of the unknown keep you from embarking on your dream.

Chapter 14

Solo RVing

"If you think adventure is dangerous, try routine; it is lethal."

~ Paulo Coelho

I travel solo in my motorhome and at every RV park I pull into, I find several other solo RVers. It used to surprise me how many solo RVers I would meet, but now I take it for granted. They are male, female, young, and old. They are in big rigs, small rigs, and everything in between. The one thing they have in common is that they all seem happy with their RVing lifestyle.

Solo RVing is exciting, challenging, and full of amazing experiences. One of the things I like about solo RVing is that I can change my mind and plans at any crossroad. The decisions are mine to make and the consequences are mine to bear.

Security

One of the major concerns for many people who travel alone, especially women, is security, which is a valid concern, but not one that should keep you from hitting the road. Lock your doors, use common sense and if a place doesn't look or feel safe, remember that your house has wheels—leave.

When you're camped in a state park or a commercial campground, you're not around riff raff. Even if someone tried to break into your RV, you could start blowing your horn or screaming and that would quickly bring more help and bring it faster than if you screamed or called 911 when living in a traditional house or apartment.

Finally, I have two things that give me peace of mind when it comes to safety and security—one is a 38 and one is a 9mm. You may prefer Mace or pepper spray.

In other words, with a little common sense and reasonable precautions, you're safer in an RV than you would be in most houses or apartments.

Loneliness

People ask me, "Do you ever get lonely?" There's a difference between loneliness and solitude. You can be lonely in a crowded room, or you can feel great solitude out in nature all by yourself.

Whether you consider yourself to be an introvert or an extrovert will have a lot to do with whether you want a lot of time by yourself or a lot of time being around people. We all need some of both, and we change some from time to time. We are not always completely one way or the other.

As for loneliness, one RVer explained it this way. She said that, as an RVer, you can decide how much companionship and socialization you want to have. One thing is for sure: RV parks are happening places. They are not lonely places by any means.

Here's how to prevent loneliness and isolation
First of all, stay in contact with the people you already know and care about—at least, the ones you want to keep a close relationship with. With email, cell phones, Skype, and a little effort, it can be done. I'm sure you would like it better if they would take the initiative and call or email you, but if they don't, there's nothing keeping you from calling or emailing them.

Some of your previous relationships will not survive. They were based on factors that have changed. What did you have in common with these people—work, church, hobbies, they were neighbors, etc.? Whatever connection drew you together may no longer exist, and the relationship will fade in time. That's not all bad.

Some of your old relationships will survive. It's not like you dropped off the face of the earth. You will still see them from time to time. You may find that you are staying in touch more while you're RVing than you did before. It's just that you don't have as much face-time. You will be replacing some of your old friends with new friends who share common interests with you.

How to adjust to being alone without feeling lonely

Since you know that you will have more time to "do your own thing" when you're living the RV lifestyle, make sure you have things that you look forward to doing—reading, writing, hiking, working on projects, etc. That way you can look forward to having some alone time.

I like to have time alone to work on my projects with no interruptions. I'm a lot more productive that way. I work as long or as late as I want to, and I take a nap when I want to. I'm usually up and doing things by 7:00 a.m., whether it's working on a project (writing, doing research, etc.) or hiking. Whatever I do, I like to start early (with a cup of coffee, of course).

RVers are a very friendly bunch, but they also respect your privacy. It's kind of an unwritten rule that you don't usually knock on the door of an RV unless invited to do so (although most people don't mind). What all of this means is that you have a lot of control over how much alone time you have. Everyone needs some alone time—some people need (or want) more than others.

If you want some alone time, you can have it. On the other hand, if you want to meet people or talk with someone, sit outside in a chair and almost everyone who passes by will speak. Then you have the option to speak and go back to reading your book or you can start up a conversation. Of course, taking a walk is a sure way to meet a lot of people in the RV park.

If you have a dog, you can soon meet almost everyone in the RV park while you're walking your dog.

Seven other things for a solo RVer to consider

After you've conquered security and loneliness, there's not much else to be concerned about as a solo RVer, but if you really need a few other things to think about, here are seven things you should do or at least consider—and by the way, these things are important for all RVers, but they are especially important for solo RVers.

1. Get active in RV forums.

There are lots of RV forums and most of them are broken down into topics. The advantages of reading and participating in forums is that you will learn a lot from reading the answers to other people's questions, you can get your own questions answered, and you can make a lot of friends.

Below are my three favorite RV forums (plus some others). All of these forums are broken down into categories, and all three of them have a section for solo RVers.

- Rv.net/forum This is one of the most popular forums.

- RV-dreams.activeboard.com This is a link to the very popular, RV-Dreams.com forum hosted by Howard and Linda Payne. You'll find lots of discussion threads where solo RVers are discussing their fears, triumphs, and questions about traveling alone.

- iRV2.com/forums This is a link to the iRV2.com forum. Ask your questions and there will be several solo RVers with real-world experience who will quickly answer them and share their experiences.

- In addition to the above forums, search Google and find a forum for owners of the brand of rig you have. If your rig is popular enough, there may even be a forum for the model of rig you have. Spend time reading several of the posts on the forum you find. Bookmark it and go back to it frequently. It's a great way to learn a lot about your rig. One of the best things about the forum is that any time you have a question about your rig (like "Where is the fuse for the brake lights for the toad?"), you will find the forum to be a great source of information. Since you will have this support group (so to speak), you won't feel like you're traveling alone.

- LifeRV.com Click on the link to the Discussion Forum at the top of the page. This is my new website and, although the Discussion Forum is not yet as popular as some of the others, I think you will find it interesting. If you have questions, I (along with others) will be happy to answer them.

2. Make copies of all of your important documents.

For peace of mind, it's a good idea to make copies of all of your credit cards (both sides), your driver's license, passport, Social Security card, birth certificate, etc. Keep a copy hidden in your RV and leave another copy with a friend or relative.

3. Read your RV manual and know your rig.

This is important and a lot of people don't bother to do this. I agree that most RV manuals leave a lot to be desired, but spend the time to find out what information is included. Also, learn as much as you can about your rig. When you buy it and someone is going over everything with you (and they will), be sure to video the demonstration. If you're buying it from an individual, write his name and phone number down and keep it with your RV manual and other information. More than likely, there will be a time when you would like to call him and ask a question.

Also, keep a file of all service and repair records. This will be helpful and will increase the resale value when you can show a prospective buyer all that has been done, and that routine maintenance has been performed on a regular basis. I recommend that you also record the date and amount of time you run the generator. It needs to be run under full load for at least 30 minutes once a month.

The more you know about your RV the more secure and in control you will feel. Know what all of the gauges and electronic readouts and lights mean. If you're a female, don't fall into the old-school thinking that you can't do certain things.

4. Get a GPS (and know how to use it), plus have a set of maps.

A GPS is handy to have, but make sure you fully know how to use it and can take advantage of all of its features. I also recommend that you have a recent road atlas as a backup.

5. Consider caravan traveling to start with.

When they are first starting out, a lot of solo RVers like to travel in a caravan with other RVers. It's a fun and safe way to travel. In fact, a lot of RVers like to travel this way even if they're not solo and not new to RVing.

By the way, I recommend that you join the group RVillage.com (it's free to join) and while you're at the site checking it out, check out the caravan group at the link below:

Rvillage.com/group/557/caravan-connection

6. Attend rallies.

Another great way to meet people and learn more about RVing is to attend one or more rallies a year. I usually attend at least two a year. Some are educational rallies and some are just fun get-togethers. Howard and Linda Payne at RV-dreams.com sponsor several rallies a year, and Escapees RV Club at Escapees.com sponsors several rallies a year. It normally costs $60 a year to join Escapees. Sometimes they have a half-price sale going on and you can join for $29.95 for the year.

7. Hide an extra set of keys in a little magnetic key box under your RV.

Make sure it's in a secure, but not obvious place. Coming back from the bath house at 10:00 p.m. and finding that you are locked out of your RV could make you feel frustrated and a little concerned about security.

I've only locked myself out once. Somehow I accidently pushed the lock button on the door. The good news was that the window on the driver's side was not latched. Also, it was the middle of the afternoon and there were several people around. I was able to borrow a wire coat hanger from a fellow camper and reach through the window and hook the keys that were laying on the dash. Lesson learned. Now I have an extra set of keys in a magnetic key holder that is securely hidden under my motorhome.

Bottom line: When I first hit the road, I was amazed at how many solo RVers I met. I'm convinced that solo RVers are safer when they're traveling and living in their rigs than they were in their conventional homes. And I know they're having more fun, so don't let the fact that you will be traveling solo be a reason not to enjoy the RV lifestyle.

━━━━━━━ **Chapter 15** ━━━━━━━

Have a Plan

"Adventure is worthwhile in itself."

~ *Amelia Earhart*

Without a plan all you have is a dream. You need a financial plan, a logistics plan, and an emotional plan. These plans don't have to be long and complicated. Each one can be put on a 3" by 5" note card. When you make a plan, things will start happening.

A plan needs to cover three things:

- What's going to be done.

- Who's going to do it. (Of course, if you're going to be a solo RVer, the "who" for everything will be you.)

- The date by which it's going to be accomplished.

You don't need to put all of the details in your plan—just basically the three things listed above. If you want to add a few more details later, that's fine and might be helpful.

The important thing is to get your plan on paper with the basic information and then you can get started working on it and making things happen.

After you've put your plan together, make sure you start working on the critical things first. If you need to sell your house before you can buy your RV, by all means, make getting your house on the market a high priority.

Taking the first steps to getting rid of your stuff (not just the junk, but the good stuff too) is hard for some people. I think one of the reasons it's so hard is because when you start getting rid of your stuff, you've made a commitment to actually change your life and hit the road. It's no longer a dream at that point.

Some of the tasks in your plan can be done almost immediately, and some things will take longer. Keep in mind that some things can be done after you get on the road if necessary.

Realize that not everything is going to go according to plan. The deal to sell your house may fall through at the last minute, or the RV you had your heart set on may be bought by someone else just before you get there.

Sometimes so many things go wrong that you might think the world sucks, but keep a sense of humor, and remember what Larry the Cable Guy said, . . .

"If the world didn't suck, we would all fall off."

Financial Plan

Start with your financial plan because if you can't find a way to make the numbers work, the rest of the things won't matter.

Things you want to consider are:

- How much cash will you have available?

- Will you need to liquidate any assets (stocks, real estate, etc.)?

- Look at your cashflow. How much will you have coming in each month from Social Security and any pensions, investments, income from rental property, or other sources? Maybe it will just be your Social Security income. Do you plan to do any workamping or other work to bring in extra income (or get free camping)? In other words, what will your total monthly income be when you hit the road?

- When you know how much you will have coming in, look at the different budgets I've linked to in the book and get an idea of what your lifestyle will be at your income level.

- Will you need to buy and/or sell any vehicles? (If you go with a fifth-wheel or camper, you will need a truck, and if you go with a motorhome, you will likely want a toad. You may have one or more cars that you will need to sell.)

- What kind of rig have you decided to go with, and how much will it cost? (If you haven't decided what kind of rig would be best for you, it should be a high priority item on your plan.)

- What are you going to do with your house if you own one? (If you're going to sell your house, get this started immediately—even if you don't need the cash to buy your RV.)

- Make a list of your expected expenses (use other people's actual expenses as a starting point and then note if there are any exceptions that you will have). For example, will you be paying off any debt? A lot of people are showing $100 to $300 a month for a pet in their budget. If you don't have a pet, that could be a big boost to your budget.

- When you find that the numbers will work, it will relieve a lot of stress and uncertainty.

Emotional Plan

Some of the emotional aspects of full-time RVing were covered in chapter 13, but that doesn't mean that you have dealt with them yet. Some of them won't be an issue until you hit the road, but there are some things you need to deal with early in your planning stage.

One thing is to tell your family and friends—particularly your kids. You can bet that they will have a lot of questions—and a lot of advice. Do enough homework (and soul searching) to enable you to provide clear and logical answers to their questions. That will go a long way in convincing them to accept your "crazy idea" (as some people will be calling it).

You might be surprised. More people than you would expect are likely to be happy for you and think you're making a wonderful decision. There will more than likely be some who will think you've gone off the deep end.

The simple solution is to have answers that will satisfy you, and if your friends and family are being logical, your answers should satisfy them too. If not, remember, it's your life. In these situations I like to think about two quotes by Steve Jobs. Here they are:

"Your time is limited, so don't waste it living someone else's life."

~ *Steve Jobs*

"Don't let the noise of others' opinions drown out your own inner voice. And most important, have the courage to follow your heart and intuition."

~ *Steve Jobs*

Logistics Plan

Some of the logistics of hitting the road (mail, banking, healthcare, getting rid of stuff, setting up a mail forwarding service, etc.) were talked about in chapter 11, but we didn't lay out a plan. This is the easiest plan of all to create. All you have to do is go back to chapter 1, make a list of the tasks, and then note who's going to do them and when. Not all of these things have to be taken care of before you hit the road, but the more of them that you can get done, the easier life on the road will be.

A lot of these things are easy to put off, but I suggest you follow the comedian Larry the Cable Guy's motto for each of these things and, just "Git-R-Done."

Bottom line: Don't fret too much about your plan. You don't even have to have a plan. You can just wing it, but I think you will end up on the road a lot sooner and with less stress if you at least have a basic plan. So start now and jot down a few things on a notepad or on some index cards, and you will have a plan. You can add more details to your plan later. Instead of calling it a plan, some people find it easier to just make a to-do list. If you're having trouble putting a plan together, just make a to-do list and you'll have your plan.

Chapter 16

Make it Happen

"Men are born to succeed, not fail."

~ Henry David Thoreau

If three birds were sitting on a fence and one decided to fly away, how many would be left? If birds are anything like people, more than likely, there would still be three birds sitting on the fence. Just because one bird decided to fly away, doesn't mean that he actually did it. We decide to do things all the time, but never get around to doing them.

Don't let your dream of living full time in an RV be just that—a dream. Take action.

Three things you need to do

1. Make a decision.

2. Set a date.

3. Make it happen.

You need to do a little bit of planning, but it shouldn't take forever. I know people who have spent two or three years planning and trying to decide if they should venture out and try RVing full time or not.

If you need two or three years to pay off some debt before you can hit the road or before you can start drawing your Social Security, then it's okay to take that much time and use the time to do your research, but there's no research you can do in two years that you can't do in two months.

Make a decision

Finish reading this book (refer back to chapters from time to time if you need to). If you didn't stop and check out the links to articles and videos as you were reading the book, go back now and check out the links and watch the videos. Do this and you will have a lot more information to help you make your decision.

When it comes to making your decision, there's one important thing to do and that is to be sure to actually listen when you're discussing this with your spouse. Make sure it's something you both want to do.

I have had several people tell me that their plan was to do it for a year or two, but after they had gotten into the lifestyle, they didn't want to go back to a "normal" life. And I've seen it go the other way, too.

Keep in mind that you can change your mind. You can sell your RV (maybe even at a profit if you've followed the techniques in the previous chapters about how to find and buy an RV at a bargain price).

My guess is that, even if you decide that the RV lifestyle is not what you want to do, you probably will not want to go back to your life just as it is now. You're ready for a change. Maybe you'll want to live in a different location, such as a warmer climate, or maybe you'll decide you want to try living in one place in the winter and another place in the summer. Whatever you do, make your decision, start living your new exciting life, and change your plans later if you choose to.

Set a date

As long as you plan to live the RV life someday, it will never happen. The time will never be just perfect. The best way to make your dream a reality is to set a date.

Set a date that's realistic but ambitious. If you're leasing an apartment, when is your lease up? That could be a good date. After you set a date, mark it on your calendar, and tell your family and friends. Then it's no longer a dream, it's a matter of fact. Consider throwing a going away party for yourselves. This will make the fact that you really are going to hit the road on your announced date a reality.

Make it happen

There are lots of ways you can go about getting ready to hit the road. I know of one couple who bought their motorhome a year before they hit the road. They moved into it and lived in a nearby RV park for the year. This allowed them to get used to the idea. They packed and repacked their RV and made some modifications to it. This gave them time to get rid of all of their stuff. They also put their house on the market and sold it during the year. The day they closed on the house, they literally pulled out of the RV park and hit the road.

To make your dream come true of living life as a full-time RVer, there are a lot of things that have to be done. Everything has to fall (or be pushed) into place to make your RV lifestyle a reality. There are so many things you have to do or make decisions about that it's hard to even know where to start. It can seem overwhelming.

The way to get started is to go back to your plan that you created in chapter 15 and convert that plan into a to-do list.

If you own a house, getting it sold or rented will probably be one of your biggest obstacles. Take steps to solve this problem first. Call a real estate agent and get your house on the market to sell or rent.

Don't sit idle and wait for the house to sell. Since you've already set a date when you're going to hit the road, get busy taking care of the other things that must be done.

A word about selling your house. I know people who have had their houses on the market for two or three years and they still haven't sold them. A lot of people have an unrealistic expectation about what their house is worth. Don't fall into that trap. It's worth what it will sell for now. The main reason a house doesn't sell is that the owner has set an unrealistic price. Set your price at a fair market value (or maybe a little less) and your house will sell.

I've heard people say that they're going to wait for the housing market to rebound. If you really thought housing prices were going to go up 15% to 20% within the next year, wouldn't you be buying real estate like mad?

Put your house on the market, set a fair price, and if it doesn't sell within a reasonable time, lower the price and keep doing this until it sells or until you decide to keep the house and rent it out. At that point, get it rented.

One other thing to be prepared for is that your house might sell within a few days. I was talking to a couple at an RV park yesterday and they said they had a contract on their house three days after they put it on the market. They had to get rid of everything and vacate the house in 30 days. Normally, getting a contract on your house is a good thing, but if you're not ready for it to sell, you might just have to get ready pretty quickly.

A few years ago my neighbor had her place on the market for over a year and then finally sold it for less than she had turned down a month after it was listed. Your house is worth what it will sell for now—not what you think it's worth and not what it was worth a few years ago.

My mother and father sold their house (and a lot of the stuff inside the house) at an auction. Maybe you're not that brave, but a good auction company will get a fair price for your house. I'm not recommending that you have an auction to sell your house, but if all else fails, it's an option.

While your house is on the market, get rid of all of your stuff that you don't need—which will be almost everything. How to get rid of your stuff was explained in chapter 5. It's easier than you think.

If you don't have a deadline, you will never get to the end of your to-do list.

Not everything has to be done before you hit the road

You are not like Lewis and Clark heading off into the wilderness for two years. You can do things while you're on the road. For example, you want to get your banking set up with two banks that have branches nationwide. It would be nice if this could be taken care of before you left, but you could do it while on the road.

You may want a better (or a lower priced) car to tow behind your motorhome. You can sell your present car and then buy something else while you're on the road.

Concentrate on taking care of the things that absolutely must be taken care of before you leave. Remember, you have a departure date. If you didn't get your riding lawn mower sold, give it to someone. You'll be surprised how fast things happen when you really do have a firm departure date.

Of course, you always have the option of renting a storage unit for those items you're not ready to part with or those you would regret losing if full-time RVing doesn't live up to your expectations.

Once you've made the decision to try full-time RVing, don't waste time second-guessing yourself. Six months or a year down the road you can reevaluate the situation and if being a full-time RVer isn't making you happy, you can sell your RV and buy or rent a house or condo and live wherever you wish. You're not locked into your RVing decision permanently.

People ask me how long I am going to continue living full time in a motorhome. My answer is simple, "Until it's no longer fun."

Bottom line: You made your decision before you got to this chapter. This chapter is to show you how to make it happen. As you get closer to your departure date, it will start to feel like crunch time. There will be a ton of things that will still need to be done and not much time to do them. Don't give in to changing your departure day. If you change it once, you'll change it again and again, and the process could drag out forever.

You've handled crunch time and deadlines all your life, you can handle one more. This one is important. Make it happen.

Chapter 17

Summing it all up

"Every man dies. Not every man really lives."

~ William Wallace

By now you probably know that the RV lifestyle is for you. In your mind, you've already moved in. But as you start to think about the thousands of choices you will have to make, you begin to feel overwhelmed. I know the feeling. I've been there.

Don't overanalyze

There will always be unknowns and, as Yogi Berra said, "It's tough to make predictions, especially about the future."

Now is your chance, while you're still young enough and healthy enough to enjoy life, to make a decision with the main criteria being, "What lifestyle will I enjoy the most?"

The good part is that by reading this book, you've found out that the lifestyle that may give you the most enjoyment won't cost you nearly as much as your current lifestyle. I think you've realized that scaling your expenses and obligations back and living a totally different lifestyle could bring you a lot more enjoyment and a lot less stress than you're experiencing now.

Take the facts, observations, and inside information from someone who has "been there and done that" and picture yourself in a different lifestyle versus your present lifestyle and think about which way you would be happier. Of course, I think you've already done that.

By the way, you know that the RV lifestyle is getting popular when country singer Kacey Musgraves has a song called "My House" about RVing and septic tanks. Here's a link to it:

Youtube.com/watch?v=m1VUNkukdHM

How long can you be on the road driving your RV? I have an uncle who is 93 and he is still driving his 38-foot motorhome. He lives in Charleston, South Carolina, and has recently driven his RV to Florida and to Pennsylvania and is now planning another trip to Florida soon. He likes to go.

Things don't make you happy. Experiences and adventures make you happy

It's easier not to make a decision and just do what you've always done, but if you end up not changing your lifestyle, let it be because you considered all of the options and came to the conclusion that living your present lifestyle is what would make you the happiest. Don't let it be because you just never got around to making a decision.

My guess is that, since you've read this far into the book, you've already made your decision. Just in case you haven't completely made up your mind or you need one last bit of encouragement, here's a story that will help you make up your mind.

73-year-old solo female RVer still going strong

Shirley Walker is 73 and she travels around the country and lives full time in her Class C motorhome. If you're wondering whether she's enjoying her life or not, watch the 7-minute YouTube video at the link below and decide for yourself. To me, this video is inspiring for us old folks. You can skip some of the links to articles and videos I provide in this book and not miss the point, but I highly recommend that you stop and watch this video.

Youtube.com/watch?v=a3MvhrkbWb8

If you decide that living full time in an RV is the lifestyle for you, go for it. It could mean the start of the happiest years of your life. Take the plunge and who knows, we may meet up at an RV rally or in an RV park somewhere down the road.

I'll just sum things up by saying, **"To be happy you have make your own decisions and grow your own daisies."**

Mark Twain summarized the idea of traveling much better than I can when he wrote the following words:

> *"Twenty years from now you will be more disappointed by the things you didn't do than by the ones you did do. So throw off the bowlines, sail away from the safe harbor. Catch the trade winds in your sails. Explore. Dream. Discover."*
>
> ~ *Mark Twain*

If you have questions for me, feel free to email me at jminchey@gmail.com or go to the discussion forum on my website at LifeRV.com

If you found this book useful, please go to Amazon and leave a review.

Reviews are greatly appreciated.

Other Books by the Author

(You can find these books on Amazon)

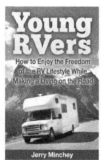

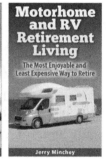

Chapter 18

Other Resources

"A man is not old until his regrets take the place of his dreams."

~ John Barrymore

This chapter contains information on resources that I think you will find helpful. Many of these links and resources have been pointed out previously in different parts of the book, but I'm including them here so you will have what I consider to be the most useful references all in one place.

I have placed the links in categories. Some of the links could fit into more than one category, but I tried to put them in the category that they best fit in. You will find a few of the links actually listed in more than one category, I did this in order to make the categories more comprehensive.

Links to information I've found to be useful

In this chapter I'm not listing all of the blogs, websites, RV videos, and RVing forums on the Internet. I'm not even including all of the ones I follow. I'm just providing information and links to the ones I find to be the most interesting and useful.

Blogs I Follow

Technomadia.com – Cherie and Chris have been full-time RVing for over 10 years. They say a Technomad is a technology enabled nomad. That's where the name of their website came from. They travel in a converted bus, that they have geeked out. Their site is a wealth of information for all aspects of RVing and especially for anything to do with technology or traveling. They have written a great book, The Mobile Internet Handbook, which is the Bible when it comes to getting connected to the Internet while on the road. You can find this book (and their other books and Apps) on their website and on Amazon.

Wheelingit.us – Nina and Paul Wheeling travel in a 40-foot Class A motorhome. Nina writes one of the most information-rich blogs on the Internet. They do a lot of boondocking and she writes some wonderful blog posts on boondocking as well as traveling and other RVing subjects. Take a look at one of Nina's blog posts, "5 Ways to Camp for Under \$500/year" at this link:

Wheelingit.us/2014/09/15/5-ways-to-camp-for-under-500year

GoneWithTheWynns.net – Nikki and Jason Wynn sold everything, bought an RV, and off they went to discover the world–at least the part they could get to in their motorhome.

They provide a lot of great articles and entertaining videos that cover their travels, equipment, and all aspects of RVing. Now they're in the process of buying a sailboat and trying that lifestyle for a while. I'm sure they will be writing articles about living on a sailboat, but the vast archives of RVing articles on their site are well worth looking at. Reading their blog is fun, enjoyable, and informative. You'll love it.

InterstellarOrchard.com – Becky Schade is in her early 30s, college educated, and a single female RVer who has been living full time in her 17-foot Casita camper for over three years. She lives on a very tight budget and pays for her lifestyle by doing workamping at Amazon, working at National Parks, and sometimes she does other gigs. She also supplements her income by writing. Her book, *Solo Full-time RVing on a Budget – Go Small, Go Now* is a great book if you're looking to get started RVing and you're on a tight budget. You can find the book on her website and on Amazon. When you visit her website be sure to click on the link to "Useful Stuff" in the top nav. bar. It really is useful stuff.

CheapRVLiving.com – Bob Wells has been living in a van for 15 years. He boondocks most of the time, lives mainly from his Social Security income plus the income from writing, and occasionally does some workamping jobs as a camp host. In addition to explaining how he lives, he also writes some great blog posts (that include wonderful pictures) about his travels and where he's camping.

GypsyJournalRV.com/category/nicksblog – Nick Russell and his wife, Terry, have been RVing full time for 17 years. Nick has written 20+ books and he writes a blog post about RVing every day. He also writes a monthly publication called *The Gypsy Journal.* You can learn more about it at: GypsyJournalRV.com.

FloridaOutdoorsRV.com/pages/top-rv-blogs – You can learn a lot from blogs and if you want to follow even more blogs than the ones I've listed here, this link will take you to a list of what is called the "Top 50 RV Blogs." It also provides a brief description of each one. I don't follow all 50 of these blogs (if I did I wouldn't have time to do anything else) but take a look at the list and see if any of them look interesting to you. My guess is that you'll find some that you like.

RV Forums

Reading forums is a great way to learn about RVing. You can see what questions other RVers are asking (and see the answers being posted by fellow RVers). You can also ask your own questions and get answers. Here are the three popular RV forums I follow almost every day.

RV.net/forum – Note that this website has a dot net and not a dot com suffix. The Discussion Group is broken into several categories (Class A, Fifth-wheels, Workamping, etc.). Check out the different Discussion Groups and you will learn a lot.

RV-dreams.activeboard.com – This is an active discussion forum with the discussions sorted by topics. Check out the "Community Chat" section, the "Buying an RV," and "RV Maintenance" sections, or others that look interesting to you.

iRV2.com/forums – This is another active RVing forum that I check frequently.

Other RVing Forums – In addition to the popular forums listed above, there are forums for just about every brand

and type of RV (Roadtrek, Airstream, National, Casita, Fleet-wood, Tiffin, etc.). Search Google and find the forum for your rig. It will be a great place to get answers to the many questions you will have about your RV. For example, "Where is the fuse for the water pump?" Your manual may not say, but someone on the forum for your type of RV will know and tell you almost immediately.

Finding Campgrounds

Sometimes I pay full price for a campsite, but most of the time I get discounts of up to 50%. Of course, sometimes I get totally free camping by boondocking on public land (where it's allowed).

There are two main ways I get the 50% discounts. First, I can almost always get discounts of 50% or more by booking a campsite for a month at a time. That's what I usually do. The second way I get the 50% discounts is by using one of the websites or Apps below:

PassportAmerica.com – Membership is $44 a year and you get a 50% discount at 1,900 campgrounds all around the country. Stay two or three nights and you've paid for your whole year's membership. I consider being a member of PassportAmerica one of the best investments in the RV world.

AllStays.com – This site has a lot of campground and travel information. You can also get their information as an app for your iPhone, iPad, iPod or Android device at AllStays.com/app

RVparking.com – This site has reviews and recommen-dations for 19,000 campgrounds. One thing I like about this site is that you get to see why people like or dislike a particular campground.

OvernightRVParking.com – Membership is $24.95 a year. They have the web's largest database of free RV parking locations in the US and Canada. Their database contains 12,783 RV Parking and No Parking locations in the USA and Canada. Search by your current location, city and state or province or ZIP code. Download PDF files by state or province.

UltimateCampgrounds.com – This site provides comprehensive information about 28,000 public campgrounds of all types in the US and Canada. They also have an app.

DaysEndDirectory.com – This site provides information about free and low-cost RV parking. To get access to this information you have to be a member of Escapees.com. Having access to this site is one of the many benefits of joining Escapees.com.

America the Beautiful Senior Pass – If you're 62 or older and are a US citizen, you can purchase the America the Beautiful National Parks and Federal Recreational Lands Pass. It's $10 for a lifetime membership if you buy it in person or $20 if you want to receive it by mail. It allows you free admission and discount camping (which is usually a 50% discount).

For example, I recently visited Curtis Creek campground in the Pisgah National Forest in North Carolina. There were 14 campsites there and only two of them were occupied. With the pass the cost was only $2.50 a night to camp and enjoy some of the most beautiful views in the North Carolina Mountains. You have to go about three miles up the mountain on a gravel road, but there is no problem getting a Class A motorhome to the campground.

You can get the pass by mail by going to this website: store.usgs.gov/pass/senior.html. To find locations where you can get the pass in person, go to:

store.usgs.gov/pass/PassIssuanceList.pdf

FreeCampsites.net – This is a free website that allows you to search for free camping places. You can enter a city and state or enter a ZIP code and see a map showing free camping places. In most cases there is information about each site in addition to its location.

ForestCamping.com – U.S. National Forest Campground Guide.

RVParkReviews.com – Information on 15,000 campgrounds and 250,000 campground reviews.

USCampgrounds.info – Information on 13,000 campgrounds that are on public land.

HarvestHosts.com – This is a great resource for finding farms and wineries all over the country where you can camp overnight for free. Staying overnight at a winery or farm is a fun experience. Membership is $44 a year, and I find it well worth the membership fee. Harvest Hosts provides you the opportunity to travel to new areas, have unique experiences, and enjoy purchasing locally grown and produced products. (You are expected to buy a bottle or two of wine or some fruits or vegetables.)

CasinoCamper.net – Most casinos will allow you to camp overnight, and many of them will even give you some free chips (they want to get you inside so you will start gambling).

If your luck is like mine, this option might end up costing you more than just camping at an RV park.

Walmart.com – Most people don't think of Walmart as an RV park, but most Walmart stores allow RVers free overnight parking. Last week I spent the night in a Walmart parking lot and there were about 40 other RVs there. They started coming in about 5:00 p.m. and most of them were gone by 8:00 the next morning. Be sure to call or check with the manager to get permission. In some locations city or county ordinances make it illegal to park overnight in the Walmart parking lots.

RVing Videos I Like

Search YouTube for the word, "RV" and you will find 3.5 million videos. Some are extremely useful and informative, some have bad and untrue information. Some are interesting and entertaining, and some are just plain boring. I haven't watched all 3.5 million videos, but I have watched a lot of them (and I do mean a lot). Below are the ones I consider to be worth your time to watch. Turn off the TV and spend an hour or so watching these videos and you will be entertained and informed.

Youtube.com/watch?v=a3MvhrkbWb8 – Shirley Walker is 73 and she travels around the country and lives full time in her Class C motorhome. If you're wondering whether she's enjoying her life or not, watch this 7-minute YouTube video and decide for yourself. To me, this video is inspiring for us old folks. You can skip some of the links to articles and videos I provide in this book and not miss anything really important, but I highly recommend that you stop and watch this video.

Vimeo.com/71385845 – I love this 7-minute video even though it's not about senior RVing. It's just the opposite. It's about a young couple and their full-time RVing adventure traveling with a small child. Take a look at it. I think you'll like it.

YouTube.com/watch?v=NGxmSGf2Kr8 – This 14-minute video shows 17 full-time RVers as they describe how they make a living while living the RVing lifestyle. If you're looking to make some extra money while you enjoy RVing, maybe you can get some ideas from these RVers.

Youtube.com/watch?v=gOUJAMNXJbk – This 8-minute video is an interview with a retired couple describing their life on the road and how and why they decided to make the transition to the full-time RVing lifestyle.

Youtube.com/watch?v=jAhBnq2pLNk – This is another 8-minute video interview with a retired couple.

YouTube.com/watch?v=ebbo800_Rg0 – This 11-minute video interview is with a young, single, female RVer. Even though this video is not about a retired RVer, if you're thinking about being a solo RVer, I think you will find her story interesting. By the way, she has now been on the road for 3+ years and is still loving the lifestyle.

TechNomadia.com/ramblings – If you like the interview style of the previous videos, this link will take you to dozens of these videos produced by Chris and Cherie at Technomadia.com.

Books I Like

With most eBooks priced at $2.99, you can get a lot of RVing information for very little money. Here are some of my favorite RVing books.

Buying a Used Motorhome – How to get the most for your money and not get burned by Bill Myers. Don't even think about buying a motorhome without reading this book. The information in this book saved me thousands of dollars, and even more importantly, it helped me pick the right motorhome for my needs and budget. You can find the book on Amazon at this link: Amazon.com/dp/14793653

Solo Full-time RVing on a Budget – Go Small, Go Now by Becky Schade. You can find the book on Amazon at this link: amazon.com/dp/B00W30OFCE or you can find it on her website at InterstellarOrchard.com. She has another book that will be available by the time you read this. Check her website.

The Mobile Internet Handbook: 2016 US RVers Edition – This comprehensive guide to mobile internet options for US-based RVers was written by full-time RVing technomads, Chris and Cherie of Technomadia.com. You can get the book on Amazon at this link: Amazon.com/dp/1530237505

Convert Your Minivan into a Mini RV Camper by William H. Myers. For $200 to $300 and a minivan, you can have an RV that you can comfortably live in. You can find the book on Amazon at this link: Amazon.com/dp/1530265126

How to Live In a Car, Van, or RV: And Get Out of Debt, Travel, and Find True Freedom by Bob Wells. You can find the book on Amazon at this link:

Amazon.com/dp/1479215899

RV Basic Training Manual – Motorhome Driving Course. Learn what every commercial driver MUST know and every RV driver SHOULD know. The book is a little pricy at $30, but well worth it. It's a 46-page manual with a lot of pictures and drawings, so it's easy to read. You can order it at this website: RvBasicTraining.com/buy-manual.html

Get What's Yours – The Secrets to Maxing out Your Social Security by Laurence J. Kotlikoff and Philip Moeller. You can get the book from Amazon at: Amazon.com/dp/B00LD1OPP6

Motorhome and RV Retirement – The Most Enjoyable and Least Expensive Way to Retire, by Jerry Minchey. (This is one of my books, so of course, I think it's a good book.) Note that some of the basic information in this book is the same as what's in the book you're currently reading, but a lot of the information in that book is not in this book. You can find the book on Amazon at this link: Amazon.com/dp/098449684X

RVing Novels: If you're looking for some great novels with plots built around RVing, I would recommend the Mango Bob series. The series includes Mango Bob, Mango Lucky, Mango Bay, Mango Glades, and Mango Key. They all revolve around a 35-year-old, single guy and his adventures as he lives and travels around Florida in his motorhome. I have read all of the books in this series and love them. You can find them on Amazon at this link: Amazon.com/dp/1889562033

RVing Groups

Escapees.com – I recommend joining this group. It's $39.95 a year and you also get membership in the new Xscapers.com group (which is mainly for the younger RVers) at no extra charge. With your membership you will receive their printed magazine every other month. I consider this the most useful RVing magazine in the industry. They also offer discounts on insurance, camping, and a lot of other things I spend money on. Take a look at their website and see if you think what they offer would be helpful to you.

Rvillage.com – This is a free website and it's a great way to keep up with where your RVing friends are and let them know where you are.

FMCA.com – Family Motorhome Association is a popular group of RVers that has been around for a long time. Take a look at their website and the benefits they offer. The cost is $50 for the first year and $40 for renewals. One of the things they offer is a program for getting great discounts on Michelin tires. They also host awesome RVing rallies. There were over 3,000 RVs at one of their recent rallies.

RVHappyHour.com – I particularly like their forums.

Healthcare on the road

Here are six websites that will give you the latest information about getting healthcare when you're an RVer.

RVerInsurance.com

RverHIExchange.com

TheHealthSherpa.com

Teladoc.com – 24/7 access to a doctor, by phone.

24-7HealthInsurance.com

Kff.org/interactive/subsidy-calculator – This is a link to a website that has a handy tool to provide estimates of health insurance premiums and subsidies for people purchasing insurance on their own in health insurance exchanges created by the ACA (Affordable Care Act).

How to find work as an RVer

CoolWorks.com – This is a free site.

CoolWorks.com/jobs-with-rv-spaces – This link goes directly to a page on the above website that probably has what you're looking for.

Workamper.com – This is a subscription website. The cost is $27 a year.

Work-for-RVers-and-Campers.com

Apps

AllStays.com/apps/camprv.htm – This is the app I use the most. With this app I can find reviews on almost 30,000 campgrounds, find locations of dump stations, find overhead clearances, and even find grades on steep mountain roads. It costs $9.99 to download the app to your iPhone or Android device.

RVParking.com – This app has almost a quarter of a million reviews on about 20,000 campgrounds. The price is right for this app – it's free.

US Public Lands – About 30% of the land in the US is owned by the government. If you've ever wanted to know where to camp free on government land, you'll love this app. This app shows BLM, Forest Service, NPS and public land boundary maps. You can download the app from Google Play or iTunes.

Other Websites

Spend an evening or two reading the articles and watching the videos you'll find on the websites listed below and you'll know more about RVing than 90% of the RVers out there. Best of all, I think you'll find the way the information is presented to be enjoyable and entertaining.

I check these websites for new information at least once a week. Most of them have a way for you to sign up and get an email message when new information is posted.

Technomadia.com – Chris and Cherie have been full-time RVers for more than 10 years. They share a lot of useful information on their site. They have a big converted bus that they have done wonders with and made it fancy and functional. Spend some time on their website and you will soon know a lot more than most long-time RVers. New articles are posted every week, and there are a lot of video interviews on this site that you will find interesting.

GoneWithTheWynns.com – Jason and Nikki Wynn have a website with a lot of in-depth articles and great information. They have articles and videos about how they make money while they're traveling, how they modified things on their RV, and they cover a lot of interesting places they have visited. Be sure to check out their website. They're con-stantly posting new and-up-to date information. They are in the process (as of May 2016) of changing from living in their motorhome to living on a Catamaran sailboat, so I'm sure their future articles will be about living on a sailboat, but you can still find a lot of interesting and useful RVing articles and videos on their website.

RV-Dreams.com – Howard and Linda have a website that's full of information and personal experiences. Turn the TV off and spend a night reading and absorbing the wealth of information they have to offer. There is also a lively Discussion Forum on the site. You can find a link to their Discussion Forum in the left nav. panel on their site.

InterstellarOrchard.com – Becky Schade is a 33-year-old, college educated, single female living full time in her RV. She does workamping more than she uses technology to fund her travels. On her site you can read her articles and you can learn more about what she does and her solo RVing lifestyle. She posts a couple of new articles every week and I think you will find them enlightening and interesting. Some of her articles are about her travels and some are about what she does, what she thinks, and her life in general on the road as a full-time, single, female RVer.

CheapRvLiving.com – Bob Wells has a ton of information on his website about living in a van. He has lived in his van full time and traveled for many years. And, yes, he lives mostly on his Social Security. Check out his website and see how he does it.

Rvillage.com – This is a great site to use to keep up with friends you've met on the road. Where are they now, where will they be next?

Motorhome.com/download-dinghy-guides – Some cars can be towed with all four wheels down and some require that you use a dolly. At this site, for $1.99, they offer a downloadable guide, The Guide to Dinghy Towing. They have a different guide for each model year. If you already own a car you're considering towing, be sure to check your car's owner's manual to see if it can be towed with all four wheels down.

What RVs have recently sold for:

PplMotorhomes.com/sold/soldmenu.htm. The people at PPL Motorhomes sell about 4,000 motorhomes a year and they show you what each one actually sold for. They also always have a huge inventory of used RVs for sale. Most of them are on consignment.

RVSchool.com – This is a great RV driving school. George and Valerie Mayleben have been running the school since 1991 and they have been full-time RVers since 2006. They teach you to drive in your own motorhome. Take a look at their schedule and see if they're going to be offering training at a rally near you. They offer substantial discounts at most RV rallies.

Use Yelp.com to find recommended local services – dentists, restaurants, auto repair shops, computer repair shops, etc.

There are thousands of good sources of information on the Internet (and, of course, thousands of sites with information that's not so useful). The links I have provided in this chapter are to the RVing resources (books, forums, videos, apps, and websites) that I use the most and the ones I think provide really useful information. I highly recommend you take a look at all of the resources that I have linked to in this chapter and throughout the book.

If you have questions for me, feel free to email me at Jminchey@gmail.com or go to my website at LifeRV.com to learn more about the RV lifestyle or post your question in the Discussion Forum on the site and you will get answers from me and other RVers.

Bottom Line: If you're just starting out as an RVer (or considering becoming an RVer), realize that there is a lot to learn in order to safely and economically enjoy the RV lifestyle. Check out the links in this chapter and you will be well on your way to being an informed and experienced RVer.

About the Author

"A forward-looking, active engagement with life is critical to growing old well."

~ Dr. John W. Rowe

Jerry Minchey is the author of several books. He has a Bachelor's degree in Electrical Engineering, a MBA from USC, and an OPM degree from Harvard Business School. He worked for NASA on the Apollo moon mission, and worked for many years as a computer design engineer. He has written four books on the RVing lifestyle, he holds five patents, and he is a private pilot with an instrument rating.

He has owned several engineering and marketing businesses. He is semi-retired now and is the founder and editor of three Internet subscription websites:

www.LifeRV.com

www.MarketingYourRestaurant.com and

www.SearchEngineU.com.

As an engineer and a business manager, Jerry looks at problems from a logical standpoint as well as an economical and financial standpoint. He has written 10 books following this format of analysis and presentation.

That's the approach he took when he analyzed the pros and cons of living full time in an RV on Social Security income.

He lives full time in his motorhome and spends the summer months at different places in the North Carolina mountains and the winter months at the Florida beaches and on the Gulf Coast of Florida. He also makes several side trips throughout the year to rallies, music festivals, workshops and get-togethers. He says, "Home is wherever I park it."

Index

Made in the USA
Las Vegas, NV
12 January 2021